I0473215

WHY QUALIFIED PEOPLE

DON'T GET HIRED

OR STAY

WITH THE COMPANY

(Based on an Employee's

Perspective and Experiences)

Molita Powell

Copyright © 2012 Molita Powell
All rights reserved.
ISBN: 147823511X
ISBN-13: 978-1478235118

DEDICATION

To those who are underemployed and unemployed, and seeking full time employment.

To those who cannot afford to go to college and those who don't think college is for them.

To those who feel stuck waiting for someone to retire in order to move into a new position.

To those who are hoping their next job will turn into a career.

I wish you success.

Acknowledgement

Special acknowledgement goes to Mr. Don Baker my former co-worker, photographer and good friend of almost 20 years.

Thank you to Pat Kimminau and Bernard Walwyn for your continued support and encouragement.

CONTENTS

Contents

PROLOGUE

As the economy changes, we see the role of the company and its leaders change to reflect a new vision. The result is a revolving door where the number of employees who exit is greater than those allowed re-entry.

Who can ignore the local and world news about the increasing unemployment rates everywhere? News on the radio and online continually remind us of the state of the economy; how many jobs were lost each week, each month versus how many new jobs were created during the same time period.

People who have been working for years at the same company, or may have just changed jobs are now a local and national statistic of the unemployment rate--perhaps through no fault of their own but a result of unfavorable decisions made by long trusted decision makers and industry leaders.

It was reported that many of the recent layoffs consisted of highly qualified workers who were having a difficult time finding new employment. Some people may be taking the much needed break and started looking for new employment only when their unemployment compensation was close to running out. This may account for the length of time they remained unemployed.

Admitting that times have changed is no cliché. Most of us can recall our experiences going through the motions from getting laid-off and the process of looking for new employment. We remember what it was like each time starting as a new employee and observing the differences in leadership styles across the various industries.

We observed the manner in which the managers and supervisors interacted with the employees, the amount of attention they gave, when the leaders interacted and under what circumstances. We then make the connection as to why so many qualified applicants are not getting hired. After all, they have what employers need and are looking for now. Why are they not getting hired?

Unemployed workers are reading self-help and how-to books, and following the step-by-step instructions to prepare them for their next work opportunity. They are attending workshops and joining support groups to network. They go to job fairs, meet with hiring managers and leave resumes with companies looking to hire. Still, they remain unemployed.

Why do some careers have a higher turnover rate than others? How do companies determine who stays and who gets the pink slip? Is there a hint of inequality that goes into the decision making?

Does this same inequality determine who gets the job, how much they are paid and the amount of visibility they get within the company?

This book is meant to change our internal dialogue when we become unemployed, whether voluntarily or involuntarily. Included are some insights for the unemployed and underemployed who are actively looking to get back into the work force or looking for a new challenge. Know there are no short cuts, quick fixes or easy streets to get back to being employed.

There are some things we have no control over. We need to recognize what we can change and proceed accordingly. Take the initiative to manage your own career. Utilize the free resources available to get started. Connect with your network of friends and find the motivation you need. Take a break before jumping back into another position.

Remind yourself that getting laid-off from one position is not always a negative. It can be a humbling experience the first time around or if you've been unemployed for an extended period of time. Use the time off to re-group and take inventory of your current job skills and experiences. This is your opportunity to decide whether you want to continue in the same career or choose another path. Once you've made your decision, act on it.

THEN AND NOW

The online Wikipedia Dictionary defines employment as 'A contract between two parties, one being the employer and the other being the employee.' The online Meridian Dictionary gives an additional meaning as 'Being an activity or the like that occupies a person's time.'

In this book, qualified people are also referred to as talented and high performers. They include anyone who has worked in the same position long enough where they can leave and work with another company in the same or similar industry, utilize their skills, knowledge and education to do the same or similar type of work with little or no supervision.

So many of us invested a lot of time and money in our education in hopes of getting that one job where we can put all that knowledge and skills to good use. So is there any wonder that we want to be selective in our choices of employment and employer?

We look for jobs within a certain geographical radius and perhaps a more specific location closer to home, the downtown area or a shopping area. We may choose an area close to a school or university, or closer to our kid's school.

In other words, the location has to be convenient. We put the same thought process into choosing the places to work, the size of the company, the various departments and the type of products or services that make up their core competency.

Well, that was a very long time ago when we had options. We would target the company within our primary area of study and apply there. We would submit the job application along with our resume and a cover letter via air mail or fax, and then wait. Here we were taught that if we did not hear back within a reasonable time after applying, we should follow up with the Human Resources Department and inquire as to the status of our job application. Sometimes the response would be promising.

Back then, we were able to have a conversation with the person doing the hiring and discuss our qualifications over the phone. We received insights as to whether we possessed the skills and knowledge that matched what they were looking for. Here, we could also find out whether the position was still open, whether there were additional positions opened or if they had anything where we could be a good fit. It may not be the ideal position, but it got us in the door to learn those skills for which we were lacking.

The other practice that employers did was to hold on to our resumes for future needs. Back then, one can count the number of applicants applying for the same position.

There were times when companies would have to extend the advertising period until they had enough qualified applicants from which to select for an interview.

It was not uncommon to be notified by mail if the position was closed, if we were not selected for an interview or for the position for which we interviewed.

Fast forward to today. We submit our resumes online and we wait, and wait, and very rarely do we bother to call to check on the status. Why? There are so many more applicants just like us applying for the same position and we apply to so many places, some unknown.

We would hear employers say today that they would get as much as 400 applicants for one position. That would be 399 "Dear John" letters sent, or 399 email replies. All we can do is keep applying until we get a call, any call.

We are putting in a lot more mileage to go to the new job. We are working in jobs we've never done, and that are not even related to our hard earned college degree. Why do we do this? We do this because our choices have become limited. There are fewer jobs available for the number of qualified applicants actively going after the same positions.

So now, we have to be willing to be flexible and to compromise in some areas. Sometimes, we even have to make sacrifices. We have to be willing to take the pay cut, drive the distance and work the unfavorable shifts if needs be. It's a matter of extreme necessity that we become open to make these life adjustments. Consider the consequences when we decide the job is too far out or the pay is not quite enough for us to maintain the lifestyle we had come to enjoy.

Have you checked the news recently? Do you know how many qualified people you are now competing with for that job you are still on the fence wondering if you should take or not? Do you know how many people would not hesitate for a second to say "Yes, I accept the offer"? Do you know how long some of these qualified people have been waiting in line for a call back or even a job interview?

Many people have had their unemployment compensation run out or close to it. People can't afford to be as selective anymore to turn down any offer that finally came their way.

If you were lucky enough to hit the jackpot and get a job interview, it would mean your resume passed the appearance and content test. Every job hunter must have that all important resume. It should be clean, well-organized, easy to read and brief.

When companies receive hundreds of resumes to filter through, you want yours to be eye-catching for the right reasons. Is the person doing the screening able to scan your resume in under a minute and determine whether it's worthy of a second opinion and for consideration?

When preparing your resume, consider what you want them to know about what you've accomplished over the years, and your potential. It may not always be what you wrote on paper, but how it's written. Are you familiar with the saying, 'it's not what you said, it's how you said it'?

Many people would write what they think the employer want them to write. There is nothing wrong with that if you can show support for it.

It's not uncommon to have several versions of your resume. In fact, it's recommended that you design your resume to the position for which you are applying. Chances are you may be a Jack or Jill of all trades. However, you do not want to show them all off at the same time unless you are writing your autobiography, and that will be after you get hired.

Focus on the skills the position requires. Highlight your skills which closely match the qualifications, especially if your experiences span across several business types. If however, you held several positions in the same field of manufacturing, food service, health care, real estate or in whatever industry, highlight them. Be brief in your descriptions and be specific. Use bullet points if necessary. Your experiences should show consistency, longevity and expanded knowledge of the industry.

There was a time when interviewers wanted to know the short-term goals (within the first year) and the long-term goals (5 to 10 years) of the prospective employees. These goals showed that we were interested in staying with the company for a long time. Then, it was easier to collaborate with the immediate supervisor to meet some of those goals.

Today it's difficult to say where we would like to be in the next 5 to 10 years since no company is immune to closures or downsizing.

The interview questions today look for competencies and skills set to determine experience and expertise. Companies want to know how engaged you are in the company. The more engaged you are, the greater the likelihood you will stay with the company. This may or may not always work in the favor of the potential employer or employee.

There are so many variables now that job hunters need to be aware of when trying to find a job in almost the same way as the employers who are looking to hire. Today we have to look at how liquid the company is and how long they've been in business. After all, we don't want to get hired by Company X today only to be laid off tomorrow. Or, get hired and not be able to receive equitable compensation and benefits due to cut backs.

We can never hear too much or too often how important it is to be prepared, both physically and mentally. Know what you are looking for and be prepared to present yourself first and foremost. That is the first thing you are judged on by the interviewers and the person at the front desk. Their opinions count in deciding whether or not you get hired to join their team. You lose points for being late so make sure that 'Be on-time' is on your to-do list for the job interview.

We see a lot of interstate and intrastate migration of qualified professionals and sub-professionals across state and county lines searching for any job they can get. Some immigrants return to their home country or travel north to try their fortune in Canada. These folks are in touch with the reality of the job market and know that companies are moving jobs to where it's more economical to operate. Therefore, if you need one of those jobs, you have to be willing to travel to where they are located.

The current economy has left the unemployed facing such financial hardship that some may be more willing than others to take a cut in pay. Prospective employers know that this willingness does not always translate to accepting the low pay. The ones who do accept are more likely to continue looking for higher compensation and will leave as soon as they do.

PART I

THE EXTERNAL ROLE

THE ECONOMY

If you were to ask some of the people who have been unemployed for a while the reasons they have not been able to find full time work, you will get answers that are similar. They will tell you the economy is slow. The job market is bad and there aren't a lot of companies hiring at the moment.

An unemployed worker will tell you we are in a recession. Their working neighbor may tell you the economy is showing signs of recovery. Where the economy is at today can mean different things to different individuals.

It's easier to point to the external influences that are preventing us from being where we want to be. Today, this is more true in Greece than in the United States where the U.S. economy is experiencing a slow period of recovery. In Greece, the situation is dire with an unemployment rate of 25.1% as of July 2012.

Wages are getting slashed everywhere and the experienced workers are migrating to neighboring countries that are looking for workers with their skills set.

The U.S. economy and the job market are slowly recovering with an 8.3% unemployment rate as of March 2012. The employment report for September showed the unemployment rate at 7.8%, a drop from 8.1% in the previous month. Compare this to almost four years ago when we were on edge as the unemployment rate was threatening to reach double digit heights, unless something drastic was done. The U.S. President Barack Obama cared enough about the direction the economy was going to make the tough and unpopular decisions to prevent further economic erosions.

Yes, many questioned the auto bailout, the bailout of Wall Street companies and the banks, but it kept the doors of these businesses open and kept workers on the job. In so doing, some of the local businesses were able to regain some confidence in the economy to maintain their current staff levels, re-hire previously laid off workers and add to their work force.

Banks and other businesses have had to tighten their purse strings to increase their capital reserves. To accomplish this, they reduced their current staff levels and delayed major decisions to add new ones pending the outcome of the next general election or just waiting for their competition to make the first move.

The carrot has been dangling for a while now around the energy market, but there haven't been a lot of takers. There's a lot of talk about energy innovations. The need is there for additional and cleaner sources of energy.

There's a greater need to create new jobs. However, there are risks associated with not having any success measures for energy companies and for anyone wanting to penetrate the clean energy market.

Instead, companies are taking extreme precautions and looking at Solyndra, for example, who wasted the opportunity to lead the way for other energy companies to open up new and larger markets. Perhaps the government loan guarantee was not a motivator in their appeal to the right market, with the right product and at the right pricing to allow them to repay the loan. Instead, Solyndra went bankrupt.

We also have manufacturers of clean energy vehicles. At a time when gas prices were escalating, the demand for electric vehicles was increasing, and there was a shortage.

Do these energy efficient vehicles deliver what they promised? Once the tax incentives have all expired, would consumers be able to afford to purchase these vehicles? Would there be enough of a demand to take advantage of the current supply or to sustain market growth for energy efficient vehicles?

Is there still an opportunity to open up new jobs in the energy market? Would eliminating the government subsidies for companies entering the energy market allow them to find creative and sustaining financing to bring their innovations to market?

Economists have a difficult time predicting the direction of the economy with accuracy in ways the meteorologists try to predict future weather patterns. Perhaps the only thing we can predict about the economy is that what goes down will come back up again.

Sometimes our best response is how we react to and affect change, and prepare ourselves for future ones. We can look at historical data and current trends to forecast future needs. With these analyses, new policies can be implemented in hopes of opening new markets to create new jobs.

How can we maintain a balanced economy at the same time we are importing more products and exporting jobs and services? How can we regain our confidence in the economy when we continually look to the President of the United States and the government to open new markets and create new jobs, instead of looking at ourselves and what we can do?

Do we truly expect the President to pressure companies to hire locally and prevent them from shipping jobs overseas? Have we forgotten the words of President Kennedy? When it comes to the economy, we have to be looking to ourselves first for the solutions.

THE JOB MARKET

Experienced auto workers, for example, are not getting rehired by the same companies that laid them off even though there are open positions which they can fill. A lot of these workers started working in manufacturing jobs at a young age and right after high school, and some continued with their family's tradition working the same jobs.

They worked their way up through the production line and into leadership positions. Some may have been working the same line for years. However, these workers are not considered skilled if they did not receive the proper education to learn about the manufacturing industry.

We have workers who did not see the necessity of getting additional education while they were being well compensated for the work they were currently doing. As a result, they got left behind with the job market changed.

If companies are not investing in these workers to provide the type of training that will take them to the next level, then their workforce will be made up of low-skilled workers.

Still, some manufacturing companies are not able to find workers with the desirable skills to hire. The ones they laid-off were trained to do repetitive tasks. These workers may have moved away, like many others, to where they can find alternative employment or have accepted other work.

In the event any of these workers were to be rehired, they may get less than what they were once paid, and will be starting again at the bottom.

Companies are not willing to pay the cost to train new and existing workers. They know that they can get workers that may already be trained and at a much lower rate, in a different country. Companies also fear the workers will go to one of their competitors for higher pay after they received the training. Here the company that paid for the training will not see a return on their investment. Would this be one reason why so many manufacturing jobs are leaving the U.S.?

Unemployment compensation is an earned benefit for the person unemployed and it helps them take care of their financial responsibilities in the interim. Does extending unemployment compensation beyond 26 weeks and up to 99 weeks benefit anyone in the long run? What effects do the extensions have on the economy and the job market? What do companies say is the reason for them not hiring? We see a lot of "Now Hiring" signs posted and the Job Wanted ads are full. But why are the positions not getting filled?

There was a time when one of the requirements for receiving continued unemployment compensation was that the individual attends some form of job training or re-training to get back into the workforce quickly. The State Unemployment Department once offered training and would recommend additional training where needed. This made it easier for an individual interested in learning a particular trade to receive the necessary training.

We see today that these training opportunities are no longer being offered, or the training is based on available funding. Private training is not cost effective for someone who is receiving unemployment compensation as their only income source. As a result, we have a shortage of skilled workers at the same time demand is high, and the job market remains sluggish.

Unemployed workers need to be motivated in their job search and not get discouraged. What if the State Unemployment Department would make it a (mandatory) requirement for unemployed workers to have finished some form of skilled training in order to qualify for an extension of their unemployment compensation? The training would be offered at a reduced cost or free to make it attractive and more affordable.

The type of training can be up to eight weeks long and may include training in customer service, medical billing, mechanics, accounting, equipment operator, etc. One would then qualify for the extension after perfect attendance and successful completion of the program. The amount of training would be aligned with the minimum requirements for hiring.

Here the hiring company works in partnership with the unemployment department and the training institutions to lay out the needs of the company, the knowledge and skills they require in order to hire.

The trainees would be guaranteed employment. Along with the guaranteed job placement, there can be stipulations wherein the new employees must remain with the company for a minimum amount of time to allow the company to recoup its investment.

At the end of the probationary period, additional training and compensation can be offered to the trainee. The trained worker would then be motivated to stay on the job longer, which in turn helps the economy to recover through job retention.

THE COMPANY

Companies are looking for incentives to hire and with the recent extension to the Payroll Tax, we are hoping that this will help reduce and stabilize the number of layoffs, and add new jobs.

There is a greater need for workers to receive both on-the-job training and specialized training to meet the minimum job requirements to get hired. We know that companies are reluctant to offer training unless the employee has time already invested in the company. However, companies need to find the balance between maintaining a talented and affordable workforce during these challenging economic times.

What else may be keeping qualified workers from getting hired? Another trend we are finding is that the senior workers are remaining in jobs past their retirement age, not as volunteers but as regular, full time employees.

Some may continue working out of necessity to compensate their social security retirement benefits income, to accumulate additional savings before voluntary retirement, while others wait around to collect their full pension benefits. Yet some may be working to keep their health insurance coverage, to be around others and maintain a set daily routine.

Regardless of the reasons, the longer these baby boomers continue working, the longer the employees who have been waiting in line to move into those positions have to wait. At the same time, if the qualified workers are not willing to wait for the positions to be vacated, they will go elsewhere.

There are some companies with a mandatory retirement age to maintain a knowledgeable workforce while others would offer incentives to those who are close to retirement, to retire early. Some school districts offer incentives to teachers close to retirement to reduce their operating budgets, but this reduces the qualified staff.

Companies should be asking themselves what types of employees they are attracting. What message are they sending when the vice presidents and senior officers jump ship with golden parachutes to go work for a competitor or claim a need to spend time with their families just when the company is struggling financially?

We see employees getting laid off or put on work furloughs while the officials are voting for and approving pay increases for themselves. At the same time, the company cannot be boasting high net returns and refusing to increase salaries.

What kind of commitment or productivity can be expected from employees who believe at any time their jobs will be eliminated or transferred overseas?

This type of inequality causes employees as well as the general public to lose face with these companies. There is a tough lesson to be learned from the way companies treat their employees that result in them losing money, and eventually going out of business. Companies should be aware that qualified and talented workers would not work for or stay employed with them if their reputation is less than favorable.

A company's culture carries with it a reputation. Like brand loyalty, customers and employees need to feel good about what they are getting for their time and money. We know employees feel good and appreciated when they receive praise, and will exercise their option to either stay or go elsewhere when they don't.

Companies are trying to be the biggest and the most powerful in their industry. We see Southwest Airlines lose its number one ranking in customer service which they held for 18 years, right after their merger with Air Tran. Southwest Airlines may see this as business as usual, while Bank of America is hoping for a break to stop its bleeding.

Companies need to take responsibility for those they choose to hire to represent them and make decisions on their behalf. Too often we see company leaders making decisions from spreadsheets, presentations and the results of employee engagement surveys that directly affect the lives and families of the employees, and without any regards for the consequences of those decisions.

Is there any wonder why there's so much distrust with corporate America?

It's encouraging to see the Directors, COOs and CEOs of some corporations and even City Mayors go undercover and work side by side with their employees, and become one of the guys, if only for a day or week. They are getting their hands dirty while learning firsthand what their employees think about the company and its leaders.

They see the results of the decisions they made that filtered down to the employees and which were not always positive. However, their willingness to admit their failures, right the wrongs and hold town hall meetings with the employees helped turn around the employees' morale and improve their company's reputation.

Some of the *Undercover Bosses* found they were doing a lot of things right and the employees were proud to be working for the company. The CEOs offered to mentor the employees who stood out and expressed their loyalty to the company in spite of their personal and professional struggles. These employees were promised a higher position if they choose to stay with the company.

This experience provided the companies with firsthand information as to why their productivity was low, and why their employees were not engaged.

Companies with leaders who are passionate about the company and recognize that the employees are the ones who helped make the company great, are the ones to survive in economic downturns. The companies that don't listen and respond to their employees' concerns will become a memory once the economy recovers, and are the ones you will find on the list of "The Worst Companies to Work For."

Companies play a direct role in growing the economy. Whether they are creating new jobs or hiring new workers, or offering incentives to attract and retain existing workers. It affects the rate of unemployment.

COMPANY WORKSHOP SUGGESTION

Problem--Steady decline in company revenues.

Cause: Reduced demand for products.

Goal: Investigate possible reasons for decline and determine best actions.

Discussion Items:

1. Are there new (competition) companies entering the market? Are they local or out-of-state?

2. Is there a need to add to and update the product lines?

3. Solicit feedback from customers regarding customer service, product pricing and quality.

4. Increase marketing efforts to get new customers and bring back the ones who left.

5. How are the company's products priced compared to its competitors?

6. Was there a recent product price increase?

7. Has the cost of production and distribution increased?

8. Are products getting to the customers on time?

9.   Are orders getting filled on time?

10.   Do we have the right staff in the right positions?

11.   Will the company have to reduce its production staff to reduce costs?

12.   How many staff will be affected and at what levels?

13.   How willing is the company to make one decision at the expense of another?

14.   How much time and notice will the company give before taking action? Will the action be immediate or in phases?

15.   What is the expected cost savings of immediate staff reduction?

16.   How quickly can the company introduce new products to the market?

17.   Would the remaining staff have the expertise to develop new products and take to market?

18.   What is the total loss in revenue for each of the past six months?

PART II

THE LEADERSHIP ROLE

LEADERSHIP STYLES

Diversity in the workplace today goes beyond Affirmative Action. The face of diversity is no longer limited to race, shades of skin color, or sex. While these factors are still at the forefront, they extend to the various styles of management.

We know there should not be a difference whether the team leader, supervisor or manager is male or female. But, is there a difference in their leadership styles? Female leaders may be more people-oriented and relaxed. We see more female leaders in lengthy, casual communication with employees. Male leaders may demonstrate and act more authoritative. They lead with a clear vision and focus on results. Does this explain why there are more males at the top of the corporate ladder? Regardless of the leadership style or gender, employees want the combination of both.

You may find a number of research and studies that explain away the behavioral styles of leaders, but in today's working environment employees are looking deeper.

The style of hiring and leading teams has changed over the years, but not the need. Employees expect leaders to be knowledgeable and fair, to lead effectively, collaborate with them, listen, encourage, reward, and be available. Instead, we see more managers not accepting responsibility for their managing.

The new manager may know the business as a whole on a higher level, but not the specific area they are now assigned to. They work on assignments for upper management and have limited communication with the employees, except for required weekly team meetings.

Because the manager is unable to provide the day-to-day support the employees need, it reflects on how the meetings are led, the information shared and the length of the meetings.

We see managers chosen to lead teams, sometimes multiple teams at once, based on their availability and current position leading other teams. And, how much money they make for the company. The result is a leader with little or no knowledge of what the new team does, and a lack of focus on mentoring.

Leaders who are not subject matter experts can benefit from collaborating with their subordinates to compensate for their lack of knowledge. By letting the employees be the trainer, the leader has an opportunity to learn what the team does, their current needs and where they (the manager) can be most useful to the team. The manager will not be adding value if they fail to participate in this effort.

It was the standard at one company where I worked that the new supervisor, just like the new employees, would sit with each employee to find out what they each did, what systems and resources they interacted with to do their jobs. Yet, I have seen where managers choose not to participate in learning what their employees do.

There can be no employee accountability when the manager doesn't know what the team should be doing or are doing.

How effective can a manager be in their leadership role when they are not engaged with their employees? The end result is a manager who falls short in their authority to organize the right employees to accomplish the right tasks required within their role. And, whose focus is not on achieving results for the company or its customers.

Can you imagine what the employee reviews are like? Some managers may prepare department goals versus individual goals. Managers who fail to do one-on-ones are more likely to give low review ratings to cut employees out of a pay raise or bonus. The good news is these managers do not stay where they are long, and do not go far.

Maybe it's time to add another question to the list to ask the prospective employer. Wouldn't it be equally helpful to know more about the skills and experience of your new manager? What is their relationship with the team like? How do they motivate the employees, and is the team motivated? What would the employees say about them? What is the culture of the company and of the team? Do they ever request feedback from the employees about the managers?

When the process that keeps us employed is broken, it remains broken for a long time. Managers ignore the needs of their employees and the employees ignore their job responsibilities.

Employees who have been working with the same manager or the same company for a long time may feel the need to pucker-up to remain in the manager's good graces and employ. These employees have not known or experienced any other leadership style of management with which to compare. They also have no expectations from their manager to be an effective leader.

Management—
Part of the Problem
or the Solution

It may have been around the time of the technology stock boom when many companies were filing IPOs that the shift in management changed more towards investor reporting. Leaders are now publicly responsible for the success and failure of the company they manage.

The leadership of these companies is under tremendous pressure to report positive numbers or have a good explanation for any unfavorable turns, along with both immediate and long term action plans to recover losses.

There was one company I worked for a while back and there was the open push to meet quarterly numbers. Often, this required each department to lose a body before the quarter ends in order to make that happen. The quarterly shuffle continued and the company struggled publicly until it was no more.

When Greg Smith published his letter of resignation from Goldman Sachs, it sent signals that proved nothing had changed on Wall Street. The companies who were bailed out with tax dollars must be held accountable for how they utilize the funds. It's difficult to say whether they should have been left to find ways to pull themselves out of the debacle they created by themselves. The decision is debatable, and the outcome shows little change in behavior.

The corporate culture, focus, leadership and reputation of companies like Goldman Sachs have changed, but not for the betterment of their clients and customers. The goals of these companies are to make lots of money for their investors and report positive earnings, by any means necessary.

William Cohan wrote of the corporate culture of Goldman Sachs years ago and noted the change from trading to long term investments, and the company taking on a lot more risks for its clients than any of its few remaining competitors. Perhaps the lack of options is the reason investors stayed with Goldman Sachs and not for the quality of its leadership or customer service.

Well, we know that Greg Smith's letter of resignation did not fall on deaf ears. In fact, the day the letter was printed in the New York Times, shares of Goldman Sachs stock fell painfully.

CNN had an online poll where they were asking 'Would you work at Goldman Sachs?' No surprise that the majority said 'No'. There are still a number of people willing to work there. The poll didn't indicate whether these were individuals currently employed at Goldman Sachs, have been accepted for summer internships or not a current employee.

It is my hope that the leadership style and culture, or whatever made Facebook as successful as it has been to date continue to work in its favor after it becomes a publicly traded company. Facebook may be the company to watch and see how management adjusts to shared decision making and now having to report to the additional investors and shareholders.

Is it possible that the corporate culture--whether they are publicly traded and have to report to investors and stakeholders--affects how much ongoing training and mentoring that employees receive, and the quality?

Most employees would know within the first six months of working with the new manager whether they will stay. The manager therefore has the responsibility in the beginning to create an environment for the employee to want to stay. If the manager isn't taking the time to motivate and develop the employees, they are not contributing to the vision of the company.

Employees are like children and need both structure and procedures to follow, to guide them to success. Like parenting, leaders don't have all the answers and are not expected to know everything. Employees want to know that their leaders are committed to their personal and professional growth, and improvement.

Managers need to be setting clear expectations and deliver them to the employees so that everyone knows what they should be doing. When you have employees walking around and asking for something to do, that's a clear sign of a lack of expectations and individual goals.

The manager needs to know the employees on an individual level to assign tasks and assess work performance.

Know their strengths and weaknesses. Know what motivates and challenges them. Give them choices and options. Provide feedback that is timely and meaningful to keep the employees motivated.

Employees should not have to wait until during the exit interview for someone to ask what motivates them or what it would take for them to stay. Is it possible that managers do not ask those questions because they don't have a response, and do not want to admit failure?

As the manager and leader, you are given a range of authority not limited to what's necessary to lead the team and to accomplish assigned goals and responsibilities. This authority affords you the flexibility to do some things that may fall outside the range. An empowered manager will not limit themselves with boundaries but will extend themselves to better the team.

What happens when managers choose to hide behind the corporate policies and not be flexible? If in exercising your authority will make you the hero of your team, why not take advantage of it? Employees are looking for their work hero. Why not let that be you?

Demonstrate you are the best fit to lead the team and show them that you know how to take charge and be in command at all times. Show your willingness to go the extra mile for the team to keep them motivated, productive and happy. Promote your team to other departments and let others know what each team member does.

Remain professional, positive and enthusiastic when you interact with the team. Allow them to feed off your energy.

Know that if you are not willing and able to wear the shoes or fall in step with being their leader, they will find one elsewhere.

Managers need to utilize the one-on-one conversations to identify any warning signs that the employee is no longer engaged and may be considering an early exit. The better the relationship with the manager, the more likely the employee will open up and stay. A lack of credibility will have the opposite effect.

Have you ever noticed that when employees are not receiving the right support from their manager and have a lot of idle time they begin to discuss how much they are underpaid and demand additional compensation? The employees who are self-motivated seek out additional training for their career development. Managers need to value and inspire all the employees. Listen and act on what employees say they need to stay.

The rate of turnover is greater when career needs are not met. 'One of the main reasons employees leave is because management isn't meeting their needs' (Cottrell). Jennifer Robison also identifies one of the predictors of turnover as 'the immediate manager' indicated by 17% of individuals who change jobs.

Individuals may not cite their manager as being the main reason for their leaving when asked. As a result, companies continue to spend money to recruit and train employees for the same position, who then leave when their needs are not met.

Can You Afford the Best?

There is a large pool of highly qualified people looking for employment as a result of company closures and downsizing. Employers would like to hire these workers because of the vast amount of experiences, skills and knowledge they possess. Their ability to multitask is attractive to companies that have had to downsize and are looking for new employees who can assume multiple roles and learn the business quickly.

How willing are companies to pay for these experiences? Or, is the company looking for fresher talents and lower salaries? And, are they taking advantage of the current state of the economy and the desperation of unemployed workers to find new employment by paying the lowest salaries? Is there a tagline next to the company's name that says 'We pay less for Jobs'?

If the goal of the company is to hire the best of the best, and the brightest, then why are there so many unemployed, qualified talents? Why are these talents the ones who get the pink slips when downsizing, while the ones with lesser experience remain? How concerned are companies about this brain drain of their workforce?

We notice in schools across the country that teachers are taking advantage of early retirement options. These are the experienced teachers that everyone knows and love. Teachers know that with their qualifications, they will be able to find another job where they can continue their passion.

Unfortunately, their replacements are often recent college graduates who need time to prove themselves while building relationships with the students, teachers and parents.

Other young talents are forced to bounce from job to job because they are not being developed or given challenging assignments. Their skills and ability to learn quickly are not utilized. As a result, companies miss the opportunity to take advantage of their fresh ideas and creativity that can increase their efficiencies. The result is a high rate of turnover with many of these talents accepting positions outside of their expertise.

Employees who know their worth and value to the company will move on if their performances are not recognized or compensated. There is no motivation in working harder and not being rewarded for it.

How attractive are companies making themselves to qualified applicants? What types of benefits do they offer and how do they compare with their competitors? Are companies doing a good enough job to develop and retain employees after they've gone through advanced training? Is there a clear path to reward high performers? Do they have a voice and if so, who is really listening?

Do the employees feel challenged or are they over qualified for the positions they are currently assigned to? How effective are the skills of the employees being utilized compared to the needs of the company? Are they being identified with the possibility of opening new opportunities for them?

The company needs to look at what programs, if any, they have in place to identify and keep their talented workers with the company. Are there any ongoing training and development for existing managers to improve their leadership skills?

What about the employees who are interested in moving into leadership positions? How long would they have to wait? Does the company have any flexibility or willingness to open up new positions in order to retain these talents?

Companies need to make it a part of their ongoing program to let the employees know of all the opportunities available to them rather than relying on them to find out on their own. If the employees have to leave the company for career advancement opportunities, it means the company has failed the employee.

We see so many managers who are overwhelmed with how much work they have to complete within a short period of time, yet they refuse to delegate to the employees. This is not an issue of confidentiality or where no one else can be trained to do the task.   This is about fear and control.

What do you think your chances are of getting hired by this manager if you are experienced?   If you do get hired, what are your chances of being assigned to work on special projects? How much visibility will you have within the team?

These managers don't want to hire people who know more than they do. When they do, the manager may be reluctant to ask for their assistance and would instead go to someone else, or spend overtime searching for the information themselves.

They would prefer to hire employees who will do as expected and not try to improve what's already in place, or make suggestions. In other words, these managers don't want their employees to think. They would rather have them work quietly with their heads down and push paper.

This may be signs of personal and professional insecurities.   The manager may feel that if the new employee with the expertise starts fixing everything that needs fixing, there will be nothing left for them to do. They may also feel they are in competition with the employee who can see what's wrong and can empower others to do the right thing.

We can still find a few people who have been working with the same company for 25 years and more. The reasons are about the same for what kept them there. It may be a lack of other opportunities outside the company and whereas some were able to move around in the company, they developed a comfort that made them choose to stay.

What I also found, which is quite apparent, employees in specialized professions such as accounting, construction, real estate, law and medicine tend to make a lifelong career out of what they do, and are more likely to remain at the same company. These workers are empowered and require less supervision. They have access to ongoing training and professional development.

In *Tabatha's Salon Takeover*, one Salon saw its income and clientele dropped significantly when half the Stylists walked out and took their clients with them. Still, the owner did not make any of the changes or responded to any of the requests made by the other Stylists, as to what they needed in order to stay.

As things grew worse for the Salon, Tabatha Coffey was called in to help identify the real issues. Tabatha worked with the owner to implement the changes and operating procedures needed to turn the Salon around to keep the doors open, and prevent the other Stylists from walking out.

The U.S. Bureau of Labor Statistics reported the leading cause of employee turnover is a lack of appreciation. As much of 65% of employees do not receive recognition on the job.

Employees are a company's best asset that can make or break the company if those assets are not valued and developed. Managers should value their employees who take the lead and require less supervision. Value the employees by including them in discussions and in the decision making process for tasks that they will be required to perform.

Recognize employees who consistently perform at their best, not just in theory and in blogs, but in practice and share the moment with the rest of the team.

Managers should be in the know as to who the high performers and the low performers are. Use this knowledge to give feedback accordingly. When giving feedback, consider the timing. Employees will respond favorably to accolades given soon after the achievement. If there is too long a delay in recognizing the achievement, it would have the same effect to the employee as getting no recognition. The purpose of the recognition will be under-minded.

What if the feedback was intended to modify or improve a certain behavior? What are the chances of obtaining the same level of performance again from the employee? What about the other employees? How committed would they be to step up their performance for you the leader? Will they continue to trust you enough to do what you ask?

No matter how long an employee has been with the team or how motivated and hard-working that employee is, if they are not given positive and constructive feedback they will lose their momentum.

Employees need validation from the manager to keep their self-confidence high, or they will soon be looking around for other opportunities where they feel more valued.

The manager's feedback should be specific not just 'keep up the good work' each time. I had one manager who would say the same thing each month they had to present the team's accomplishments. The manager never took the time to ask for input, and as a result never had anything to present. The only thing said about the team was, 'Thank everyone for doing a good job.'

Employee Engagement Versus Employee Empowerment

I recalled a time in the late 1980s when employers would attempt to empower their employees, when there was a clear path for upward mobility. The high performers were singled out by their immediate supervisor to be their replacement. The supervisor would mentor and coach the employee. In these situations, the supervisor was also being developed to move into a new position.

This was the trend that continued up to around the turn of the twenty-first century. Today, we see that employee empowerment has been replaced with employee engagement and takes on a different, more passive meaning. Supervisors and managers are moved into lateral positions more often than into vertical jobs. The upward movement now takes much longer because people are staying in those positions longer.

Employee engagement measures what an employee thinks and feels about the company as a whole and their jobs. It focuses more on the employee's emotional commitment to the team and to the company. An engaged employee will speak highly of the company, but would they recommend the company to their friends for employment? Are engaged employees happy employees?

Empowered employees contribute directly to the organization's bottom line. They are self-motivated, productive and results-oriented. Managers empower employees through mentoring and development, and paying attention to the needs of the individual employee.

Companies pay a lot of attention to the results of the employee engagement surveys to tell them what they are doing right, where they fall short and where improvements need to be made. They also look to see how their overall percentages measure up against their competitors and other businesses. After all, if the competitor's employees are happier and more 'engaged', then they will be attractive to the employees who do not feel management is doing enough to keep them around.

At the same time, the company often misses the mark in terms of where the employees say the company falls short and the main reasons for the low overall percentage ratings. The reasons outlined for the failure of managers to be effective leaders are not explored. As a result, the right remedies do not get implemented to ensure that employees are motivated to stay with their current manager or with the company. The company fails to implement the right actions.

Employers want their employees to be engaged; to engage themselves. But, if being engaged means giving employees some control over what the department does, how willing are managers to give up the controls or share some of the department responsibilities? How willing are companies to go the extra mile to provide employees with what they need such as flexible work arrangements, trust, career development, challenging assignments, open support and visibility?

How much do employees know about what the company does and who the top leaders are? Or, is the CEO able to go undercover in the company without being recognized? Do employees have what they need to feel excited about coming to work every day and be productive? Or, are they already checked-out and barely there?

Companies need to position themselves to be proactive, and be ready and willing to respond to employees' need to be engaged and empowered. Employees need recognition for their efforts. They need to be kept in the loop as to what's happening within the company and not wait to hear on the national news.

They need to know how they can contribute to the direction the company is moving. What employers need to know is that employees will not complain about the things that are not within the company's immediate control to fix. Employees are concise about the inhibitors to their engagement and while they continue to do what's expected, they lose motivation.

One way of getting the best from employees is to empower them. Don't just delegate tasks for them to perform. They need to be held accountable for the results or lack thereof. This is what will drive and motivate them to perform.

Remember to give immediate feedback and encouragement to keep the team going. Don't forget to say 'thank you' to your employees when they've completed a special task for you.

I was watching an episode of *Undercover Boss (Abroad)* in which the CEO was working odd jobs at the various company sites. At one location, there were more employees assigned to do the same cleaning job alongside middle managers. The employees and the managers were vocal about how they felt about their job, the company and their pay.

At the next location, there were fewer employees doing the same job, with no middle managers. The manager in charge got rid of the other managers, paid the employees more as incentive for doing more work. The employees were empowered because their pay was directly linked to their job performance. They received immediate feedback and knew what they needed to do to increase their weekly take-home pay. These employees enjoyed their job, the pay and the company, and it showed.

The roadmap to empowerment for any new employee starts with the trainer and the type of training they receive. It's easy to sit and look over someone's shoulder to later mimic what they do. However, the quality of the training one receives is in what's being communicated, not the length of the training period. The trainer should be someone who is knowledgeable, self-motivated, empowered and resourceful.

The communication should be informative and includes an introduction of the company, the products and services provided, as well as how the company makes its money. The focus should be directed towards accomplishing the goals of the department and the company, and how the responsibilities of the other employees together make that happen.

Once the trainee understands what's expected, they will feel empowered and in a better position to retain the information being given. The trainer then needs to create a sense of urgency in the tasks that need to be completed, to spark excitement and curiosity. In so doing, the new employee learns the right questions to ask after developing their own critical thinking, and will return the next day to learn more.

The initial training should not include step-by-step instructions as it forces the trainee to remember just that. This creates anxiety, fear and the need to write everything down which interrupts the flow of the training. You don't want your new hires checking the company's intranet site the first day looking for something that looks more challenging.

First day training sets the tone for what the job is really about and the expectations. At some point, the manager needs to check in on the training and do follow-ups to ensure the new employee is getting everything they need to complete assignments on time.

Being empowered means you are focused on meeting your assigned goals. If these goals were a collaborative effort with your manager, they would be more aligned with the vision and mission of the company. The level of productivity increases for empowered employees. They receive mentoring from their manager which in turn improves their commitment to the company.

WHAT MOTIVATES

David Cottrell refers to employees as 'Over Achievers'. Employees who are self-motivated no longer aspire to be like their manager. Instead, they want their manager's job. They feel they can do a better job managing, communicating and responding to the team; better at executing and developing relationships, and with more confidence.

No matter how many fresh baked cookies and bagels the managers bring in for everyone, or parking lot style picnics the company have for the employees, there is no substitution for individual attention. That is, giving credit when and where credit is due.

There are lots of things the company and the managers can do to get employees excited and motivated which do not cost money. So why isn't more being done? Does the company supports the manager's decision to do nothing or is it the manager's ego on display?

It's no mystery that we are all motivated by money. The question is how much money and for what reward. Money, however, is not at the top of the list of what motivates most employees. Bonuses, for example, are taxed and the amount of the cash award may not align with the accomplishment.

Employees love to earn rewards. The reward can be in any form such as working half a day, free and reserved parking, gift cards or even real cash (tax free). The key is individual recognition. Of equal consideration is the process by which the employees qualify for the rewards. The process has to be clear to motivate; one that is attainable and the reward distributed fairly. Include the employees in the planning process and listen to their input as to what motivates them.

AON Hewitt did a research on the Trends in Global Employee Engagement and found that 'The largest engagement drop is in how employees perceive performance management.' For the three years that the study covered (2008-2010), overall engagement was down especially in areas of Leadership, People/HR Practices and Communications.

The 2010 employee engagement scores compared drivers for the regions of Asia-Pacific, Europe, Latin America and North America. For each of these regions, the top engagement driver was 'Career Opportunities'. All except North America ranked 'Pay' as fourth out of five engagement drivers. For North America, 'Pay' was not among the top five drivers.

This further shows that what motivates employees is not always money, and money will not buy their loyalty.

The needs of employees have changed and employers can no longer treat everyone the same.

Employers can create multi-level positions in addition to junior and senior level job titles and positions to implement a structure for career growth and pay opportunities. This is also a great way to differentiate job responsibilities with related pay.

These would consist of positions within a position. For example, a junior level position may include a hierarchy for entry level, intermediate and senior positions. There are some job titles that include first, second, third, fourth and fifth level title extensions.

Each hierarchical level should be clearly defined and includes a set of responsibilities and related pay ranges for each position. Any required education and training along with a timeline to move to the next level should be outlined. Include the descriptions of any special requirements for advancement to the next level beyond the basics, and how each performance will be measured. Discuss the changes with the employees and get their feedback before rolling out.

Once the new procedures have been implemented, the manager needs to set up interval times with the team and with each employee to give and receive feedback. Employees will feel better about being rewarded for their contributions and performances. The low performers will either pick up the pace or be left behind.

Along with rewards, employees need to be held accountable for their actions, and the consequences for their inactions need to be agreed upon.

Employees want to know that they are working towards accomplishing a goal that improves their job satisfaction and help them achieve professional success. Employees will do what is expected of them if they know the importance.

If an employee is told to do XYZ, they will only do XYZ. If the manager explains why XYZ is necessary and how it will be utilized, the employee now has a better understanding of the expected outcome when task XYZ is concluded. They will then be motivated to do what it takes to obtain the desired results.

Leaders need to do more to share what they want the employees to accomplish. One mistake that leaders do is to assign more work to the top performers because they know the task will be completed timely and successfully. Unfortunately, these employees have a different take on it and don't exactly feel that getting more work should be the reward for doing good work.

It's hard to see the positives when the other team members are not carrying their share of the work load. Eventually, the top performers will become more like the average performers. Employees want their compensation to reflect what they do. It becomes difficult to stick around when the low performers are getting the same pay.

Some companies have adopted incentive-based pay models and pay-for-performance. If the manager is not meeting the needs of the employee regardless of the compensation and the job market, the employee will leave.

What do you typically find employees doing when they are not motivated and do not have enough work to do? And, what happens when their work environment is not conducive to the standard of work they are expected to perform and deliver? They play games and post to their online social network using their cell phones. Or, they would pay bills, shop on-line, share recycled dumb-dumb jokes and socialize.

What managers don't realize is that when you have one employee walking around socializing, they are taking time away from someone else. This means you have at least two people not being productive.

Managers need to set clear and firm expectations for everyone to know what their responsibilities are. Be consistent. Provide oversight and hold employees accountable. Acknowledge good performances and achievements, not just the little things, and reward accordingly. Delayed acknowledgement and reward will fail to motivate.

One thing that managers who fail to motivate have in common is that they are not subject matter experts and do not show any willingness to want to learn. Some of these managers may be new in their role and did not participate in training with the team. Others may be wearing too many hats and are always in reaction mode, and not being proactive.

They may be preoccupied with running and preparing reports for upper management and just don't have the time to lead the team. These managers hold back praise and recognition. They may not want to give awards because no process has been established for giving them. Others may think they are giving up some control when they give praise.

When your manager doesn't know what you do on a daily basis, you are not rewarded or acknowledged for your skills, input and contributions, or it's done in private.

Employees need visibility and a manager in whose leadership they trust.   Employees may not always be clear as to what the vision or mission of the company is, but will follow the lead of the manager if they have clear roles.

It can be a challenge for managers to determine how to keep their top performers motivated and interested in the job when they continue to exceed expectations.

One way of accomplishing this is to assign to them an ongoing project. However, in order for the plan to be effective the manager will need to show open support by discussing the project with the entire team and ask them to cooperate with the new project leader.

An example of an ongoing assignment can be to create and keep updated a Best Practices Manual for all the different tasks performed by the team to accomplish their job responsibilities.   The best practice for the task will be chosen by the project leader from among the contributions received from the other employees. The project leader will be responsible for the implementation.

This activity gives the employee the spotlight. It improves the operating processes for the team, and it's a great team building effort. Here the top performer feels empowered and included.

Managers have another challenge on their hands and that is in trying to motivate the different generations.   This is more than another check-off on the diversity check list. Today we have the baby boomers working with the Generation Xers and Ys.

Their needs are all different and so is what motivates. In order to manage the different generations, the manager needs to understand them. Here is where the one-on-one meetings can eliminate the stereotypes and biases that exist within each group.

Managers need to understand the individual personalities in order to know how well any two or three will work together, and under what leadership style. Know that they each have their own set of expectations from their manager. The Generation Ys born between 1982 and 2005 are tech savvy and great at multitasking. They have strong work ethics and grew up getting a lot of praise. This means they are smart and self-motivated, and will expect positive feedback from their manager.

The issue with the Generation Xers born between 1961 and 1987 is that they are waiting in line for the baby boomers to retire. However, the baby boomers are not quite ready to pass the torch. As a result, they are not too keen on training the Generation Xers to push them out either. Their knowledge does not get passed on. This may be a sign of senility and insecurity.

The Generation Xers have learnt to be resourceful and efficient in finding ways of getting the job done. And while the baby boomers, born between 1946 and 1964, are basking in their own self-importance and blinded by their inability to perform their own responsibilities, the Generation Xers are becoming more innovative and creative in developing themselves.

Managers need the skills to motivate these diverse work groups and to create an environment of trust and synergy. The baby boomers will have to leave eventually and the manager will need to have a Business Continuity Plan in place to ensure a smooth transition. The manager can implement an immediate plan to begin cross-training the entire group and allow for work rotations. This decentralizes the heart of the knowledge and makes it easier for anyone planning to leave.

Employees will appreciate their manager sitting down with them to set individual goals, both personal and professional. The plan should include a timeline to accomplish each goal. The goals may be based on previous feedback given by the manager or a peer review with added suggestions on how to improve upon a task, such as additional training. Employees will be motivated when the right message is conveyed and the take-away from the manager is positive.

THE MANAGER'S
BLIND EYE AND DEAF EAR

ABC News Nightline aired their first visit to the Apple Manufacturing Plant at FoxConn in China, in March of 2012. The workforce there was as young as 17. Hard to ignore was the netting surrounding the factory and the living quarters that FoxConn was forced to install after about five of its employees had jumped to their demise.

The reason for the suicides given by one of the employees was not because of the then 12-hour daily shifts that they worked to exhaustion, but because of management.

I started watching *Restaurant Impossible* and have seen a pattern of behavior for the reasons these restaurants were failing. Many of the restaurants were within one and three months of closing their doors even after the owners had pumped upwards of five hundred thousand and over one million dollars into the restaurants over time.

The new owners, made up mostly of family members and friends, bought the restaurant as an investment and for their retirement. For others, ownership was passed down to the next generation.

Most of the owners had absolutely no experience in managing a restaurant. One owner even put her young sons in the kitchen to cook. None of the kitchen staff members had any formal training. Their only training was from the previous owners and cooks.

Whenever someone spoke up with suggestions for process improvements in the kitchen or in the front of the restaurant, they were ignored.

Sometimes the staff didn't know who was in charge since everyone did what they wanted. There were a lot of blame and resentment to go around for the lack of respect for and from the employees.

The owner/manager would be watching their staff chewing gum in front of the customers, eating food off their plates before packing and even ignoring the customers when they walk through the front door.

There was no process for re-ordering food. Needless to say, a customer may order a dish from the huge menu and would be told they were out of a food item. The servers also could not tell the customers what ingredients were in a dish they had never tasted.

The manager didn't know how much they were spending on food, or for overhead, but they knew how much they were losing each month. This was money they borrowed from friends and family.

There was one family that used their child's college fund and another took the equity from their home, while others used their retirement funds to put into the restaurant to keep it afloat.

Clearly, these owners were in denial and had been for a while. They refused to believe that the food they prepared and served the customers was a problem and the reason customers were not returning.

Before Robert Irvine, the host, can attempt to fix the failing restaurants, he first had to identify all the problem areas and hold someone accountable. The accountability usually falls on the owner/manager. By then the owner/manager had lost control of the restaurant and staff, and had pretty much given up on them.

The staff had no respect for the manager and there were no consequences for their actions. Put all these together with the owners deeply in debt, and you get bad food coming from a kitchen that the cook himself would not feed to his kids. Customers returned to the dated restaurants out of loyalty and support for the family.

These owners would scream at Robert for pointing out their shortcomings and the reasons their business was failing and losing money. They had grown so accustomed to the dirty kitchen and the lackadaisical customer service by the servers, and family members who don't want to take orders from anyone. Everybody saw the problem but no one dares to talk about it lest it becomes their responsibility to fix.

Sounds familiar? How many times do we allow things to slide while we look the other way? Is it the employee's responsibility to speak up and speak out, or is it the manager's responsibility to see what others cannot see and fix before it becomes a bigger problem?

Managers need to take charge and handle the issues within their control and not wait for an outsider to point them out. The restaurant owner/manager cannot hold the employees responsible for the restaurant's failing without acknowledging their own failure to manage. Ultimately, the owner is always responsible, along with the manager assigned to manage and lead the team.

On the surface, families working together can appear to be an automatic win-win situation, but the failing restaurants proved otherwise. Regardless of the family dynamics and the relationship between manager and employees, and the people they are in responsible charge of, there has to be clear boundaries that everyone is aware of and more importantly, respects.

So much emphasis is put on making sure that employees get along with each other to make it easier for them to successfully collaborate on team projects and activities. There is nothing wrong with encouraging collaboration, but is it possible the relationships you are trying to forge may lead to group think because the participants believe that is what's expected? And, the manager may end up making the decision because the team has exceeded their time limit without a decision.

Does anyone believe that Donald Trump would select celebrities who all know each other and are best buddies to be on the same season of *Celebrity Apprentice*? Apart from the entertainment aspect of the show, don't you think that these celebrities are selected more for their differences than their similarities? After all, diversity is strength, isn't it?

A diverse group with varying personalities should be celebrated because they bring strong opinions and ideas that are useful to the group, and to the challenges they are about to face. Differences also promote competition. The more competitive the employees are, the better the results of their performances.

Managers need to recognize when an issue is based on a difference of personality or poor performance, and address the issue accordingly. This way the negative behavior does not get the most attention unless steps are being made to shut it down. Family members or not, managers need to always be managing and leading.

There is a reason some companies do not allow or encourage managers to socialize with their staff outside the office. This is to avoid any inappropriate behaviors and discussions that can cross the line between manager and subordinates.

When these lines become blurred or erased, the manager's ability to lead effectively will be compromised, and they will not get the same amount of respect and productivity from subordinates. This affects team members in different ways.

Often the relationship with the manager becomes a close friendship and the manager's ability to lead is again compromised. This leads to the manager failing to acknowledge and address less than favorable performances. Instead, the now friendly manager has to pick up the slack left by the employee.

The next question is why doesn't the manager delegate the task to other employees? Well, remember the high standards by which the manager is held to? They are no more. So is the respect. Employees will follow and support the managers who hold themselves to a higher standard, and who remind themselves of the boundaries that allow them to maintain the mutual respect of their employees.

Once the manager loses that respect, it's very difficult and near impossible to get the employees to volunteer to help another employee who continually falls behind on their responsibilities, while the manager turns a blind eye.

Employees will also not support the manager when half the full time staff is walking the aisles with nothing to do because they were allowed to pass their responsibilities on to the contract workers. This does not reflect well on the manager's ability to manage work levels as well as hold employees accountable for their work.

This type of lackluster leadership and oversight may stem from a lack of training and preparedness for the managerial and supervisory position. Employees expect consistency from their manager. The attitude of the employees towards the manager may result in the high performers going to another team or company.

Manager, know that your employees hold you at a higher standard and expect that you will act and lead accordingly. Employees look to their manager first for solutions. They do not expect that you have all the answers or be an expert, but at a minimum be willing to locate the answers for them or refer them to who can.

Focus on the employees and they will give you their best efforts every time. Listen when ideas are being shared and do not allow them to fall short and on deaf ears. Managers are responsible for making the work environment a place for employees to strive and want to stay. Manage and lead the team to avoid having too many people sitting around with nothing to do.

Standard Operating Procedures are put in place for a reason. They should not be prepared for show-and-tell when the outside Auditors are expected. They should be implemented and enforced. If there are no procedures in place or the procedures are not adhered to, the new employees remain green and the experienced ones become complacent.

When employees become complacent, it doesn't mean that they've lost the passion for what they do. They lose respect for the manager and no longer do what is required of them by the manager. This may be a result of ongoing and questionable decisions by the manager that contradicts the company's policies and operating procedures.

At the end of the work day, employees want to feel like they've accomplished something; like what they do matter and that they've earned their compensation. Manager, do not rob or deny your employees of those feelings. Otherwise, they would all become clock watchers and ready to go as soon as their shift ends. They will not go the extra distance with you or for you.

Managers need to know their employees and draw their own conclusions when it comes to behavior changes. Don't allow a complaint from any one employee to railroad a good relationship you have with another based on what he-said she-said. A good manager should not encourage, entertain or react to gossips and negativity from one employee about another. Doing so will only serve to enable and encourage the complaints.

If you know your employees well enough, you will be able to determine the motives behind the complaints and the complainer.

Don't feel the urge or need to confront or mediate every complaint. People who complain are either looking for attention for themselves or looking to draw attention away from them. The wrong reaction to the complaint can have repercussions for the manager for misreading and mishandling the information received, and for not verifying the info before confronting the employee.

Managers, employees know there are times when you need to show empathy to certain employees during difficult times. Show empathy for the right reasons. Do not enable bad behavior because the person is in a protective group, whether it be a disability or age group.

This does not reflect well on you as a leader capable of making sound decisions, and your staff will not trust your judgment. They will also not approach you with important issues or suggestions for improvements. You will not receive the same amount of respect.

Your actions as the manager represent the vision of the company. How employees are treated radiates to how they treat the customers internally and externally. Happy employees will represent the company positively.

Management
Accountability

What about accountability? To what extent are managers being held accountable for the success or failure of their team? Do you have 20% of your team doing 80% of the work? Or, are you more interested in the overall results rather than the individuals?

Managers are employees too. They are not always right and do not always make the right decisions. They need to be held accountable in the same manner as the employees they manage. The power of authority that comes with the position should not exclude them from this.

The CEO of AT&T Randall Stephenson was forced to take a pay cut of $2.08 million for the failed merger with T-Mobile in 2011. The actions and decisions made by the CEO caused both companies to lose money. During the merger talks, the retailers were instructed by T-Mobile to pull their products from the shelves. Instead of T-Mobile cell phones and phone cards, they were replaced with the AT&T equivalents.

This means the success or failure of any merger or acquisition comes with a huge price, including massive layoffs. It is not often we hear of the CEOs of any company held publicly and personally responsible for the losses incurred as a result of their decisions, but there are others. Again, this does not get reported often, but we hope the trend will continue to encourage and force managers to make better business decisions that affect so many in the process.

Consider one company forced to downsize due to a lack of customers while another steadily losing money when the customers are ignored. The company that is losing money may be a direct result of having too many employees not being productive, who are not interacting with or responding to the needs of the customers. Here you have money walking through the doors and having to walk right back out because no one is paying attention to it. The behavior reflects a lack of urgency, leadership and consequences.

The company forced to downsize may be a result of external influences not in their immediate control. This may include new competition from new products with very low prices. There may also be a shift in the market with some products becoming obsolete, plus delays getting new ones out in time due to raw material suppliers going out of business. This results from a failure to react to market changes and take proactive measures to ensure a steady supply of products.

In these examples, we see the opportunity for both companies to turnaround. One company is able to do so immediately through re-training, setting expectations and holding the manager and the employees accountable.

If the leadership of both companies had their focus on increasing income revenues, would we see the same results? Is it possible that having too many managers reporting the same departmental information makes it easier to lose focus?

How long will it take leaders to accept responsibility for their decisions and hold themselves accountable? Or, do they continue to point fingers at the employees for not doing as instructed?

We may find employees doing less than favorable tasks out of obligation and fear. Over time, we know that the results of these decisions will come to light and someone will be held accountable.

Are managers making the connection with the employees to make sure they share in the vision and mission of the company? Do managers value their employees or do they see them as demanding of their time and attention?

What about the team's culture? Is peer-review a part of the culture, and does that include a review of the manager?

Whether the manager is responsible for managing employees or processes, or both, the decisions they make should help the team meet their goals. The types of decisions and the manner in which they are made may be more appealing to the team than the actual results.

If companies keep doing the same thing, they will get the same results. Case in point is the latest rant by Rush Limbaugh. For the past 20 years of his career, Rush is known to be a controversial Radio Host with a large following. For at least two days in a row, Rush berated Sandra Fluke, a law student, for voicing her own concerns before a panel of Democratic lawmakers regarding the cost of contraceptives to be included in the health care coverage.

It wasn't until the companies who advertised during his show pulled their commercials, and political members started to distance themselves from him did Rush apologize, and apologized some more for his remarks.

Rush Limbaugh is known for a lot of things, and apologizing is just not one of them. Needless to say, his apologies fell on deaf ears.

Perhaps it's time for him to make a selfless contribution to the economy and let someone else waiting for a job gets one. Free speech does come with a price even for Rush Limbaugh.

Regardless of the position you hold within your company, when you are in a leadership position you are always leading. Be sure you are leading others in the right direction. How else can you expect them to be 'engaged'?

How many managers do you know with employees who do not respect them, or do not perform their assigned tasks? Remember the TV show *Restaurant Impossible*? One owner/manager and parent with small children would have to go into the restaurant at 5:00 a.m. every day to sweep and mop floors, and wipe tables because the staff went home without doing the required clean up.

Holding employees accountable includes setting clear expectations and making sure everyone knows what they are responsible for on a daily, weekly, and monthly basis.

It makes no sense for the company to assign someone as the manager without giving them the chance to do their job or to support their decisions. If the manager does not know what's expected, they cannot execute their task. In addition, the employees will not take them seriously when they try to manage.

Managers should be held accountable for the contribution they make to the company's bottom line, whether it is positive or negative. That includes hiring great people with expertise and letting go the ones with no desire to be there and are not contributing to the success of the team.

Train and develop employees to do a good job for the company and deliver results. Managers need to give employees the tools they need to perform at their best and in an environment which promotes learning and growth.

When employees are growing and learning, they are being productive. Employee productivity contributes to the mission and vision of the company and over time translates to the company becoming profitable. Managers therefore have a responsibility for maintaining the success of the company by effectively leading the employees they are put in charge of and should be held accountable when they fail. When managers fail to grow their employees, the company is adversely affected.

'Leaders and managers who fail to instill a sense of progress into the careers of their employees, do the business great harm'(Wagner, Harter).

We see the faces of managers getting younger. Part of the growing problem is that even after the new managers and leaders are provided with the required training, there doesn't appear to be any follow-ups. They are not held accountable for implementing the tools they were given to take back to their teams.

Managers may struggle with being both an employee and the leader of a team. However, that is the job they chose, and that is the role they accepted.

It is not acceptable behavior when managers willfully and intentionally choose to ignore their employees' accomplishments, and to not acknowledge their achievements. These managers may think that they have to receive recognition from their manager in order for the practice to trickle down. The result of this behavior is a high turnover within the team, and with new recruits coming more from the outside than from the inside of the company.

We know their focus and priority do not include the employees. What are the chances that this manager would have a successor trained in the event they have to leave the company on short notice? Or, are they busy trying to maintain their own job security by hoarding information and appearing overly busy?

This is where the manager needs to have a one-on-one conversation with their own manager to revisit their leadership role, and if necessary sign up for additional training. If this does not help, then the manager needs to step down or step aside as they are doing both the team and the company a disservice. This manager is not ready to lead.

LEADERSHIP
DO'S AND DON'TS

Manager, as the leader, you deserve respect from everyone on your team. However, you are not entitled to it. You have to earn it. The way you go about earning their respect matters. Don't make up new rules or target employees to discipline for minor infractions in order to instill fear in the group. The employees will not see you as being tough or authoritative. Instead, they will see through your insecurities.

On a re-run episode of *Tabatha's Salon Takeover*, I heard the manager say that he would let the Stylists fire themselves. He explained to Tabatha Coffey, the host, that he intentionally acted mean towards the staff members he didn't like and was not kind to them. He sabotaged their client's schedules. He does this to force the staff to quit.

During the week Tabatha was there, one staff quit because she could no longer deal with the management style of running the business.

What the manager failed to realize was as the person who the staff looked to for leadership, his own actions were on display. Each action and inaction was being analyzed. It took some time for the owner to build up the courage, with Tabatha's help, to put the manager on probation for six weeks. The manager felt because he was with the Salon the longest, he was holding the business together. He was wrong.

Managers need to lead by example. Leaders are made, not born. If as the manager you do not feel you have what it takes to lead, motivate and grow the team, then step aside or get the training you need to do what is expected in your role. Do not accept a leadership position if you are not committed to creating and maintaining a successful team. Managers are always being tested. Be honest. Share your past work experiences in your introduction to the team. Set expectations for the team and for yourself.

Do keep the promises you make to your team. If you fail to deliver, they will not take you seriously the next time. If you plan to take your team out to lunch to celebrate an event or milestone, you will need to follow through. Always do what you say you are going to do. If you find that you don't have the time to set it up, delegate to someone to make the necessary arrangements.

While it has become a common practice to celebrate employee birthdays, do not overlook employee anniversaries with the company. Celebrate the milestones, the accomplishments and the employees' contributions to the team and to the company over the years. Individual recognition goes a long way.

Do not act out your fear of managing to belittle or intimidate your employees. We realize there was a practice where managers were taught to not get friendly with their staff, to be tough, and limit contact as a way of demanding respect and to differentiate yourself as the leader. This is one sure way of demoralizing your staff to get them to quit. You will not gain any loyalty or respect when you act in this manner. Your effectiveness to lead the team will be brought into question. Your employees will not think highly of you and will speak negatively when given the opportunity. Your intentions will have the opposite effect.

Do not show favoritism and bias, or single out your average employees to promote because they say 'yes' to everything they are asked to do and don't question anything. No matter how much you build-up and reward these employees, you will not get anything more out of them than average. They are satisfied with doing little work and routine work. Some employees require more attention, supervision and training than others. Communicate with the team any additional training you will be giving and invite others to participate. At the same time, do allow equal opportunities to all the employees.

Do communicate new information to all the team members at the same time. Prepare meeting notes for future reference and share with employees who were not present at the meeting. Do not relay the information to a few and rely on them to communicate to the rest of the team. Employees look to you to lead and take charge of every situation, and would prefer that you communicate directly with them.   Employees may think there is something wrong with them, but more so, you.

Do not make decisions when your emotions are high. Focus on the issues and not on yourself or the team member. Stay on topic. Practice being a good listener to control your emotions. Challenge yourself to manage and control your reaction to what is being said. Once you've found your balance, others will mirror your good behavior.

Another way of controlling your emotions is to not bring your personal life to work, and do not share with your team. Your employees are not your family. Keep the relationships professional. Mention if you must, but do not discuss personal issues. Oversharing will break down the dynamics and the boundary of the manager-subordinate relationship. Once that door is open, it will be difficult to close.

Do make time management a priority when it comes to spending time with your team. Delegate some of your tasks to them if needed to free up your time. This gives them a chance to know what you do.   The team deserves your individual attention, not your excuses. Nothing can be more important than the time you spend building your team.

As the manager, you are responsible for the successes and failures of your team.   The time spent should be planned, productive and useful, and does require you to be prepared to share and discuss new information with the team. If the time is being used for team building, make sure the activity is constructive, that there is something they can take-away with planned follow-ups. Be sure to follow through on the follow-ups. Don't plan the activities for it to be another check-off on your 'to do' list as a manager. Your employees will see this as another time waster.

Do not let your responsibilities as the manager distort your judgment when it comes to chronic complainers. Identify the motivation for the behavior and put an end to it immediately. Get clued into the timing of complaints. If this is included as part of the peer reviews, this will only encourage complaints and show the low expectations you have of your employees. Meet with each employee to learn about them on an individual level. Do not rely on any one employee for this information. The information they share is likely to be self-serving.

Do know that your low performers and high performers are not motivated by the same things. Do not try to automate every process to aid the low performers. It will leave them with less or nothing to do to keep busy. The manual processes may be the only ongoing conversation they have with you, and their only connection with other members of the team. Without this involvement, how will they know you still care about what they do, and how else can you tell what they are doing?

Some employees perform better with repetitive tasks which do take time to complete. This should not reflect on them as being a low performer or, does it warrant the need to automate the task.

Do not exclude the high performers in thinking they do not need your involvement because they are meeting your expectations. If that is the case, consider raising the expectations and find ways to get involve in what they do. You do not want to be the type of manager who attracts only low performers to your team, or have your high performers begging to be rescued by another manager.

Do coach your employees to build better working relationships, improve job productivity, job satisfaction and work quality. This will allow employees to meet individual goals and show how they are contributing to the company's vision. Year-end reviews would then be more purposeful than the dreaded ratings and rankings that do nothing to develop and improve employees. Improve your own competency through coaching to obtain the desired productivity results the company expects and requires to be competitive and profitable.

Do set a standard of excellence for your team. Do not give rewards for the sake of giving them. Consider the results and the level of performance you are trying to achieve and what you want the employees to accomplish. Reward progress that is measurable.

LEADERSHIP WORKSHOPS

Problem 1: **Manager unable to connect with employees in order to get assignments completed.**

Cause: Unequal treatment of employees and inconsistent decision making.

Goal: Improve communications with each employee and be more accessible

Action Items:

1.   Communicate often and to all employees at the same time.

2.   Set clear expectations with the employees and put in writing.

3.   Hold one-on-one meetings to set individual goals that are aligned with the company's goals.   (Note to manager: Keep these meetings positive and focus on the individual).

4.   Recommend additional training for the group and individuals.

5.   Hold meaningful team building exercises.

6.   Allow each employee to lead a project.

7.   Encourage positive peer reviews.

8.   Provide constructive feedback regularly.

9.   Implement an ongoing program where you recognize and reward employee accomplishments.

10.   Involve the team in the decision making process and get their input on changes that will affect how they do their jobs.

Problem 2: 20% of the Employees doing 80% of the work.

Cause: Manager not having control over what the individual does and allows employees to choose what and how much they will do.

Goal: Need to balance the work load and distribute among the team.

Action Items:

1. Meet with all employees and communicate to them the need to change work assignments in order to balance the work load.

2. Re-iterate the department's goal and the company's mission.

3. Let the employees know how you, the manager, contribute to those goals.

4. Meet with each team member to set up individual goals and work assignments.

5. Tie-in goal accomplishments with compensation.

6. Set time intervals to accomplish each goal.

7. Agree on consequences for not meeting the goals.

8. Find out about any additional training that the employees may need to accomplish their goals.

9.   Finalize individual responsibilities and put in writing.

10.   Meet again with the team and share what each person will be doing going forward. Do not allow any changes to what have been decided upon.

11.   Ensure the department's Standard Operating Procedures manual is updated and that each employee has a copy.

12.   Schedule follow-ups to ensure everyone is on target.

13.   Hold employees accountable.

14.   Implement an ongoing program where you recognize and reward employee accomplishments.

15.   Give praise and show appreciation.

Note: It's important that everyone knows at all times what the others are responsible for. Do not allow one employee to pass work on to another without your approval. Be consistent, be firm and follow through on the agreed upon plans. Allow yourself to be held accountable for the success of the team, at the same time holding the employees accountable.

PART III

TALENTED

HIGH-PERFORMER

QUALIFIED

THE INDIVIDUAL ROLE

DOES YOUR EDUCATION MEASURE UP?

The unemployment lines are growing longer and it's taking much longer to find a job. The bar has been raised for professional jobs. Whereas some college courses were once acceptable, the minimum requirement now is a Bachelor's Degree. As a result, job seekers have to be flexible in the types of jobs they accept as well as the pay. In other words, without the right kind of education they are forced to look for new careers and different jobs.

Experience may be the best teacher, but companies are looking at your education first. The job market is saturated with college graduates, some of whom hold multiple and advanced degrees. More than 30% of adults have at least a bachelor's degree according to the *U.S. Census Bureau*. Whereas the number of new college applicants is increasing, only half of them are finishing college due to rising college costs. Nonetheless, having a college education is invaluable.

A college degree offers you more career opportunities and allows you to be more competitive in the job market.

With the student loan debt now more than a trillion dollars, how much will you be adding to it? Does your choice of study enable you to get a job or internship right after you graduate? Would you need additional training? How long will it take you to get a job? What is the job market like for that type of degree? Would you need to take on a second major or a minor to compensate and compliment your career choice in order to ensure you have what employers are looking for?

Does your passion translate to helping you earn a living? Or, are you more attracted to type of degree and the letters after your name? Consider the types of jobs available for your degree, and the earning potential. Find out which companies have college hire programs and the ones that do on-campus recruiting to re-direct your focus if needed.

Research your career path and your education. You won't go to a Mexican restaurant expecting to get authentic Italian food. Plan your college search the same way. Know what the college or university you are interested in applying to is known for. Study their curriculum to determine if the courses offered in your major field of study are sufficient and go far enough to teach you all you need to know to compete and perform the job. Visit the university if possible with your check-list to see if it's a comfortable fit for you.

Be selective in where and what you study. If ever you are not able to decide what you want to study, make a list of career interests. Narrow them down to about five. List the pros and cons of each choice. Include your passion for your choice, the salary, job market, transferrable skills, and role models. Your education is one of the best investments you can make in yourself. You may lose a job, house and car but never your education.

Select the college or university that best suits you in terms of their core learning, the location, in-state versus out-of-state tuition, curriculum, and accreditation. Visit www.ed.org and www.degree.net and check out the accreditation of the colleges and universities you are considering. Read online blogs. Visit online social groups and hear what students—past and present—are saying about the culture, the curriculum, the professors, tuition and financial aid, the available resources and facilities, events, campus life and life in the dormitories.

Pay attention to comments regarding the institutions' sales tactics or any unfavorable pressures to enroll. Colleges and universities may promote themselves based on the number of their graduates who receive employment right after graduation. What they are not saying is how many are actually working in their field of study.

Don't forget to consider the current market. Search the Job Wanted ads to see what employers today are looking for and find what interest you the most. Look to see what the educational requirements are for the positions, as well as the range of pay. Is the annual salary for the position going to be more or less than the student loan debt you will accumulate by graduation?

Plan ahead to get your money's worth. Don't go to college because you are expected to go. Once you start, plan to finish. You don't get credit for dropping out if you don't have anything to show for it, and you don't get a refund either.

Once you decide on a career and have a plan for college, work the plan. You will only know what you are good at if you follow through. If later on you decide that you want to change your area of study, don't beat yourself up about it, change it. Follow your passion and stay focused. Be sure to graduate.

College graduates and post graduates stay employed longer. They earn more money and are able to enjoy a better lifestyle. Their earning potential afforded by having a college degree can be the difference between those who can take a vacation and those who are still paying off their student loans.

On the other hand, high school graduates have limited options to move out of their economic class because they may only qualify for the lower paying and sub-professional positions. This does not include the movie stars, professional golf players and other sports stars with only a high school diploma and some college courses.

This is also not to say that you cannot move up the ladder after a number of years working in the same position. The opportunity is there, but with just the high school level education, the ceiling is lower than for someone in the same position with a college degree, and the path to the higher salary takes longer.

Additional on-the-job training and advanced training in management can help. You may be given a long fancy job title, but the pay doesn't measure up. Individuals without a college education are typically the ones affected the most when unemployment is high and when companies are doing layoffs. In other words, they are easily replaceable.

A college education is not limited to a four-year college or university. Community Colleges offer two-year degrees (Associates of Science and Associates of Arts) and certificate programs. There are specialized courses where you are given hands-on training in computers, electricity, plumbing, mechanics, welding, nursing, etc. There is a shortage and a need for these talents.

If you don't feel college is for you, consider becoming a skilled worker. There are vocational institutions available where you can learn and develop your expertise to become a Landscaper, Chef, Electrician, Musician, Artist, Painter, Tailor, Barber, Machinist, Equipment Operator, Computer Technician, etc. The requirements to gain entrance into these programs may not require you to write your life's story, but do come with a cost.

The training is hands-on, fast-paced and allows you to build your experience in less than a year. Upon successful completion of these programs, you can move right into working in a professional environment.

In addition to the specialized training you will receive, you can work towards earning a professional license and certifications. These would allow you to earn more money and be in greater demand.

If you plan to be self-employed, it would be helpful to know how to own and run a business. College marketing, business and accounting classes will go a longer way in helping you to grow your business. To remain successful, you will need to stay committed and continue learning to improve your skills.

Once you've completed your skilled training, go to www.redbeacon.com and find out how you can become a local Red Beacon Professional (in select areas) to expand your network, and start working immediately and independently as a Contractor.

The Juan F. Luis Memorial Hospital's CEO Jeff Nelson announced the layoffs of 85 Certified Nursing Assistants and the Licensed Practical Nurses. The reason he gave was that they were moving towards an 'RN dominant model for patient care' (Baur). He continued to say 'Registered nurses provide the highest level of patient care and critical thinking, and perform the full range of care services, whereas, LPNs and CNAs are restricted by law to provide fewer services.'

The positive of the layoff in this already struggling economy, is the opportunity the laid-off nurses have to complete their education to become Registered Nurses, and be considered for re-employment at the JFL hospital. The hospital planned to create a fund to aid the laid-off nurses in this endeavor.

It's unfortunate that otherwise qualified workers have to wait until they lose their jobs to be forced to finish the education they started so long ago. Too often folks drop out of college when they get a job or forego college to accept full time employment.

The laid-off nurses need to stay motivated and keep their eyes on the prize. Take advantage of the time off and finish their education.   No one knows more than they do how crucial a time this is for them to get back to work. Let the promise of a salary increase keep you motivated throughout your studies.

If you've been unemployed for at least six months after graduating with at least a four year degree, then it's time to ask yourself the serious questions. How aggressive have you been in your job search?

Are you looking for jobs only in your field of study? Have you done any follow-ups? Have you received any call backs or email responses? Are you willing to relocate? How open are you to other opportunities not in your field? If you have not received any interests, it may be time to look at your degree and the types of jobs you are applying for.

Some of you may have followed your passion and obtained a degree in Philosophy, Liberal Arts, Education or Business, for example. Know the limitations of these degrees and what jobs are available. Also, know which degrees teach you skills that are transferrable to a wide range of jobs and the ones that require mandatory training and additional courses.

In this case, do not target specific jobs and market. Instead, be open to other industries to increase your chances of getting hired. While you are waiting, consider taking specific classes to increase your marketability. Don't apply for a job solely because of the pay. The money will come later.

Some seasons may be more favorable than others for hiring. You may be competing with new college graduates who are willing to accept a lower salary to get hired. These are the seasonal jobs that college students and teens seek out during their break. Now, we have laid-off workers going after the same jobs to supplement their income.

Also, know that some companies do put jobs on hold periodically while they re-work their budgets. This is a good reason to follow up if you haven't heard from them after a while. Some companies do not hire during the Christmas season. Use this time to polish your resume and prepare to send it out the first week of the New Year.

LET THE AVAILABLE RESOURCES DO THE WORK FOR YOU

After you have updated and polished your resume, then it's time to think about where to send it, whom to send it to or even when to send it. Timing is everything. Don't just wait until your unemployment benefits are about to run out or you've drained your savings down to a mere drip, and you are in survival mode. You can't find what you are not looking for.

We can go knock on doors, make phone calls and get an immediate response. However, with today's technology, we can post resume(s) to multiple job sites and make them searchable to recruiters, employers and Temporary Services Agencies. Be sure that your resume includes some of the key words from the job postings for the types of jobs you are applying for to increase the number of hits.

Job search sites such as Jobbing, Yahoo, Hot Jobs, Career Builder, Dice, Monster, JobServe, JobSense, JobsinDallas,

TheLadders, and Indeed are just a few popular ones you can use.

The response may not always be immediate but this way your resume gets greater exposure with minimum effort.

Because the prospective employers and recruiters cannot see what you look or sound like, a lot of emphasis has to be put on the tone of your resume. Be sure that it flows smoothly, and that it positively and accurately represents who you are and what you want them to know about you.

Social groups such as LinkedIn, Facebook, Twitter and online Blogs are great tools for you and other professionals to build networks.   If you are not familiar with *LinkedIn*, it's free to sign up.   There are sections and subsections within LinkedIn which can help you to focus in on the types of positions that closely match your skills. It shows you various career options to broaden your job search and allows you to consider the possibility of changing your career.

For any career you may be interested in, LinkedIn shows other professionals within your network with similar skills. If you wanted to find out which companies have openings for the types of positions you are interested in, check out the list and follow the links to the company's site for current openings. Using LinkedIn to do your job search will show off your technical savvy.

Don't forget to check out the blogs for additional tips for your job search. You can find tips on how to structure your resume to show your experience, but not your age. For example, you can omit the year you graduated from college.

While you are online, do a search for best cities to work in and best companies to work for. Some of the popular magazines and online news websites such as *CNN Money* would publish a list each year with their top 10 or top 100 best companies to work for. These are based on what the employees say make the company a great place to work. Remember that every company would say they are the best place to work so you will need to read the employees' reviews for the other truth.

The reviews include company location, salary, career opportunities, work schedule flexibility, perks, culture, benefits, low turnover rate, company liquidity, equal opportunities, employee appreciation and bonuses to name a few, and in no particular order. These are just some things to expect from a great company. Also, do a comparison and see how the rankings of these companies change each year, and how they measure up to your current employer.

Your affiliation or membership in a professional organization should be your first place to look for new opportunities or to transition into another profession.   Let your social groups know you are ready for a career or job change, and find out what's available in their areas. Since they've worked with you in the past, they will be able to provide a good reference and attest to your skills, experience and work ethics.

Visit Vault.com for additional interview tips, tips on ways to structure your resume and cover letter, and to compare salaries and benefits.

The local State Unemployment Department is another great resource.   If you are getting laid off, some HR Departments will give you a packet full of resources you can use to help find another position.   Do what works for you, and utilize the tools relevant to what you are looking for.

At the same time, don't be afraid to try something new. If you find a new site that you like, sign up and post your resume. Think outside the flushed margins of your resume and be open to something new and challenging. You may be surprised at how transferrable your skills and experiences are to that new company or industry you've never considered before. With each time you change jobs, you are essentially changing careers while starting over—both with compensation and skills set.

Always look at the positives. Be optimistic. Get excited about the idea of doing something new and different. Don't dwell on the comfortable job you lost or the friends you've left behind. Think about the pros of the new job such as less stress, shorter driving distance and how much you'll be saving on gas alone. Perhaps you'll be getting more money and this may even be your dream job. Even if it's not your dream job, think about your financial responsibilities and how this job will help. You can't lose what you don't yet have.

For some positions, the no brainer minimum requirement is a high school diploma or the equivalent GED. Way back when, having completed some college courses would be acceptable as the minimum requirement for professional jobs. 'Some' may mean the applicant is currently enrolled in college and working towards a degree of some kind. This showed growth potential and companies were willing to pay the tab for the continuing education after you've worked there for a while.

After completion of the educational studies to compliment your work experience, you were rewarded with additional compensation and a higher position. This was not uncommon.   Companies today are thinking and planning ahead on how they can extend to you the same educational benefit, and be able to justify the budget for it.

Minimum, non-negotiable educational requirement may be a Bachelor's degree.   There are plenty of qualified individuals with this type of degree, so this is just another filter in the qualifying process. Here, the company doesn't have to pay for it—you already have. Instead, the company would only have to invest in your advanced learning, if your manager approves of it.

Companies today have their own in-house university with online courses. They can teach whatever you need to know to perform your job responsibilities. If they do not have someone well versed in the subject area, they will bring someone in to train you.

Companies are also partnering with local colleges and universities, as well as specialty training institutions to make sure you have the tools needed to perform the job. This is an extended benefit to you, especially since job responsibilities and work schedule can make it difficult to work and attend outside classes. Take advantage of it. With all the cost cuttings that have to be made across the board, companies can plan ahead by eliminating or adding to their internal training programs.

By the way, this department operates more as a cost center than a profit center. If you are a trainer in this department, be sure to always remind employees what courses are available and encourage them to sign up and show up. You have to maintain your own job security, right?

EXERCISE YOUR OPTIONS

When job hunting, ask yourself if you are looking for a job or a career. How much longer do you want to continue working before retiring or move onto doing something different? Are you looking for a full-time or part-time position?

Know what size company you are comfortable working at when doing your job search. With smaller companies you may wear several hats and these positions challenge your ability to multitask. Does this appeal to you? Larger companies are organized by departments. It affords you the opportunity to learn the business of the company one department at a time.

Depending on the size of the company you are applying to, there may be various recruiters assigned to specific job types to streamline the volume of applicants, as well as the frequency of the need. Agencies that recruit for contract and permanent positions for these companies are organized for accounting, technology, leadership, executive and administrative type positions. As you are applying, keep that in mind if and when you follow up to ask for the right person in the right department who can share accurate info with you about the position.

At the same time, it doesn't hurt to ask what other positions they have currently that the company is looking to fill. Find out what if any positions are on the horizon—not yet posted. Some recruiters may be able to share if there is a new company looking to relocate in the area or of any expansions within one of their client companies where they would be looking to mass hire in the near future. If there is only one recruiter for the company, inquire if they have any position you may qualify for based on your skills set and education. Always consider your willingness to be flexible.

Many companies rely on Temporary Services Agencies and Head Hunters to provide them with qualified workers. Whether you are unemployed or underemployed, using Temporary Services Agencies are a great way to get back into the work force quickly and find what you are looking for. These agencies are contracted by employers to fill both full-time and part-time positions, and for short and long-term contract employment.

Yes, you may have to fill out a lot of paperwork and perform a battery of tests, including a drug test, based on the type of company and the work specialty. Don't be afraid to accept temporary work assignments. You may end up getting more money in some cases to compensate for the medical benefits the agency does not offer.

Some agencies can offer industry competitive pay as well as paid vacation, medical benefits, 401K plan and other benefits after you've accrued a certain number of hours, or once the grace period expires. The *Imprimis Group* and *KForce* are two of these agencies that offer benefits to temporary employees. The medical benefits are optional and you can elect not to participate. There is a cost that you pay just like if you were working a full time position with the same coverage. Read the fine prints and ask questions before you sign up.

The real benefit of working with the Temporary Services Agencies is the on-the-job training you earn with every assignment. This is an undeniable experience that you can add to your resume and take with you to the next job. With each new contract position is the inescapable opportunity to learn new skills, new areas of the business, and to build relationships and contacts for future job hunting.

Imagine you are working in say the Marketing Department of a company with a one year contract. At the end of the contract, you would have earned one year of valuable experience which could be exactly what is needed to apply for the sales position in the same company. Warning, some agencies do not want you to solicit work from their clients when you are there or within sixty-days after your contract ends. If the contract you signed with the agency includes any of these stipulations, respect the protocol.

If you did a great job for the company, they will remember. If the company wants to hire you, they will. You can always apply after the waiting period has expired. Your manager or supervisor there can be used as a reference, with their permission.   If you find that you've taken a liking to marketing, then that can be an area of interest to pursue.

Temporary assignments allow you to sample various careers and narrow your choices to a single one. With every assignment you are in a position to learn a new skill. Take advantage of this opportunity to do just that. Know that the assignment can end at any time and without notice.   Be prepared.

I say this because there is that dreaded downside to working temporary positions. You may be given the grunt of the work from permanent employees and the work shift that no one likes. Remind yourself you are there to learn and be compensated, and that it's only temporary. Learn everything you can while you are there to build up your work experience.

Consider the Armed Forces. They offer great on-the-job training opportunities as well as college funds to continue your education both during and after you've left the service. Some companies will hire based on your military service in lieu of the required experience for manufacturing and other jobs. Take advantage of the military training, but take caution that the jobs you do may or may not transfer to the civilian world.

If you or your family are immigrants and speak a foreign language, you may have an opportunity to be a professional Translator, Linguist or Interpreter. Embrace your culture. Learn additional foreign languages and enjoy a career that involves traveling to new places and meeting new people.

Volunteering is another option available to anyone.   It affords you the opportunity to maintain your momentum by occupying your time with meaningful work rather than being at home. Note to the baby boomers. Here you have a choice of places to volunteer and you set the schedule that works for you. You may meet other people in your situation who are trying to keep themselves busy while waiting for call backs on possible jobs.

Volunteer work is not limited to the not-for-profit organizations. You can scout the Job Wanted ads and look for companies offering internships, paid and unpaid, to individuals within a specific field. This can be very appealing to someone who will benefit from a few weeks of on-the-job training.

If you were temporarily incarcerated, working for non-profit organizations and volunteering are ways to ease your way back into the work force. What better way to fill the gaps on your resume.

SHOW ME, DON'T TELL ME

Regardless of what's happening on the inside of the company or the style of management, that is no excuse to not be an active participant in your own success. No matter where you are, it is up to you to fulfill your work responsibilities in the allotted time, and in doing so learn all you can.

In the event your employment (contract) is cut short—whether voluntarily or involuntarily—you would not be one of those folks being distraught and wondering what to do next, as you would have learnt a new area of the business, learnt a new skill or improved on the ones you already had. You would have learnt a few more computer and business applications and gain intimate knowledge of the industry during your time working.   You would have also made a friend or two whom you can rely on as a good reference.

Unless you are of the type who don't like to be told what to do, don't like to be corrected and do only what is required or asked, then I would not be worried.

I have seen too many people who say they have over 10, 20 or 25 years of experience doing this or that, but their actual work performance shows differently. That kind of talk didn't work years ago because for most jobs, you had to demonstrate your ability to do the job in order to get it and keep it.

There is actually a method to the madness when you register with the Temporary Services Agencies, and have to take a speed typing test and 10-Key tests, math and spelling test or give a sample of your handwriting. Then, it was more of don't tell me what you can do, show me.

What I've found over the years is that some of these folks who are counting their years of experience have failed to keep up with the times. Some of their experiences and skills are antiquated because they never built on their initial area of study. They never extended themselves, or seek out new and additional information.

In other words, they wait to be told what to do and even when they are told what to do, they never question anything. If it's something they don't know how to do or want to do, they pass it on to someone else. They are the ones who are quick to say 'what used to happen' or 'this is how we used to do' this or that.

Don't be shocked if your prospective employer asks you to demonstrate what you've done versus you telling them. Unless you are doing data entry or word processing, the agency may accept your word for it if you tell them you can type. There are certain professions that require that you prove you can do the job before you get hired.   Actors and Musicians have to demonstrate they have the talent to do the job.

As a technician, you too have to demonstrate you can troubleshoot and fix a computer or network problem; fix a given problem with a car, an air conditioning unit or a clogged sewer line. The same goes if you claim to be a Cake Decorator, Make-up Artist or Hair Stylist. If the interviewer cannot decipher your skill level or how current your knowledge of the industry is, then you may just be wasting their time.   They will move on to the next applicant.

Get the idea?   Even if your current position doesn't require that you take the courses being offered at the company's expense, consider taking them. Did I mention that employment was 'at will'?   Don't ever get too comfortable at your job. Don't think you are too busy or too valuable to be taken away from your desk, the customers or emails, to take a class that is being offered because you think it's a class you will never use or just not interested in.   Don't wait for the stream of "Dear John" letters to change your mind.

If you are unemployed right now, you may be thinking about the past training opportunities you passed over that prospective employers are looking for you to have recently completed, and which are keeping you in the unemployment line.   Make sure your skills are up-to-date.

Recognize the Distractions

Whenever we start a new job, it becomes natural for us to befriend our co-workers. We develop close friendships which extend beyond the work place. The new, close relationships give us a reason to want to come to work each day. Some companies would ask if you have a best friend at work. They know that relationships are important and can help an employee to de-stress and can be the reason they stay with the company.

There are some relationships, however, that are not encouraged to take root in the work place. Some companies may allow spouses, multiple family members and relatives to work within the company, so long as they do not work in the same department or where one supervises the other.

While every effort is made to build relationships, there is no avoiding the ones that fall apart. This creates conflicts.

The types of conflicts may result from a difference of opinion, gender, generation, and personality, as well as a difference in leading and in styles of communication.

The personality conflict is the most dreaded. It's the one that comes packaged with emotions and misunderstandings, and tend to escalate into something larger than itself, much like opening Pandora's box. Regardless of the cause, it should be recognized for what it is. There are times when any attempt to resolve one conflict, creates additional conflicts. As such, it may be more advantageous to be accepting of the differences and find ways to work with or around it.

Some companies offer training in Cultural Diversity for the employees. This brings awareness to everyone as to how ignorance can create conflicts, and how the issues can easily be resolved through knowledge.

All conflicts should not be seen or treated as negative, and that require confrontation or mediation. Conflicts, like diversity, can promote healthy competition among individuals and teams. The types of conflicts should be identified and separated into what may be task related or people related.

The types of conflicts that relate to people come in different forms and as such may be difficult to control. Some conflicts may be distractions by one individual to gain control over another individual, or task. Be aware of employees who are distracting you from doing what you are trying to accomplish. We hear empty vessels make the most noise. That includes the folks with nothing good to say and are the ones doing the most complaining.

Their lack of professionalism and excess socializing at work show a lack of accountability and lack of consequences, in the absence of effective leadership. These behaviors are what feed the root of potential conflicts. These are your low performers who are overdue for a career change. The high performers may be creating conflicts to eliminate their competition.

These same employees are the ones that push to be your best friend. This makes it easier for them to pawn their responsibilities off to you to do so they can extend their time socializing with others. How can you justify saying 'no' to helping a friend with work?

It's important to recognize these differences and know when to step aside to avoid becoming a party to any potential conflict, or bring it to the manager's attention in order for the event not to materialize. It may be difficult to ignore the people conflicts, but sometimes that can be the best resolution as the more attention given to it, the bigger it gets.

Here, the manager needs to recognize the effects the negative behavior have on the other employees as they are forced to participate in frequent personal conversations so as not to appear unfriendly, or not a team player. When one team member creates a distraction for whatever reason, the burden falls on the other members of the team.

As this continues, employees become frustrated. They walk around on egg shells, and they lose respect for the manager. The manager is no longer seen as someone with control over the employee, but is manipulated by the employee (complainer).

It's also possible the manager has allowed the behavior to go on for so long without stepping in with corrective actions, that doing so now may result in the employer being sued for discrimination (based on a protective class such as a disability, age, sex, religion, etc.). The manager's hands become tied, and the employees are forced to accept and deal with the uncomfortable situation in which they are placed.

Another group of co-workers you want to be mindful of are the ones who appear to be highly confident. Companies look for employees who display confidence in their abilities and are the ones who get hired. Companies seek out this trait in employees to build leaders.

On the other hand, this confidence does not always translate to the expected level of performance. The confident employee may have an explanation for everything and can talk themselves and others out of any situation. They may be the more logical choice to turn to for advice, but they will only talk you out of the decision you've already made. Once you've decided on any plans for your success, stick with them.

Remember the work environment can bring out the competitiveness in everyone. Choose carefully whom you turn to for support in the work place, if not your manager.

Be selective in whom you choose to build friendships with in the workplace. Surround yourself with the types of people who would allow you to be your best and support your choices, even when they don't agree.

Learn how not to react to what is being said, to avoid unnecessary confrontations. It's important to recognize when others may be trying to discourage you from achieving your goals to build themselves up. The disappointing part of this behavior is when the manager does not recognize the conflict for what it is, and buys into it.

CHANGE IS GOOD

To improve is to change. To be perfect is to change often. Winston Churchill.

I was recently reminded we are creatures of habit. We tend to get comfortable in our work environment and with the people we work with. When the time comes to change, we are neither mentally nor physically prepared for it, and we resist it.

We have to change in order to grow and improve. Tim Tebow and Peyton Manning are two athletes who were forced to make a change to new football teams. How well they handle the change and transition into their new cities will reflect on how they adapt to and perform with the new teams.

Employees who have been working in jobs for ten years and more are least likely to seek out new opportunities. They have established work routines, and are comfortable with the duties they perform. These employees may have additional roles where they interact with everyone in the company. This includes volunteering and organizing the various company-wide functions. With this type of attachment, additional compensation takes a higher priority over career advancement.

We identify this group by their words and actions. Have you ever tried to train an employee to do a new job or teach them a new skill? Do they continually interrupt to say they don't understand or they are not getting it? Do you find yourself asking to take a break before repeating yourself?

These are the employees who you watch write down the information you are giving them, and remind them to refer back to their notes. Yet, they return to you and ask the same questions, and to be shown again what needs to be done.

These employees are the ones to test your patience every time until you are able to comprehend what they are really trying to say to you. These employees have been doing their jobs for an extended period of time and are somewhat knowledgeable in their areas of responsibility. When the opportunity is presented to them to take on additional duties, the employees appear to be overwhelmed with the new information. They request additional time and training in order to feel comfortable taking on the new role.

When employees say they don't understand what they are being asked to do, what they are telling you is, they don't want to do it. They don't want to hear or know about any new responsibilities which they will later be requested to take on.

They are satisfied with the amount of work they have to do currently and would prefer not to do anything more that will change their routine. Here the employees have successfully manipulated the situation to not having to take on any new responsibilities.

Employees who resist change will seek out an explanation for additional roles they are ask to assume, and will complain about it until it gets re-assigned to someone else.

How can one compete with these employees when their annual review shows them to be consistent in completing work assignments, and are always available to volunteer for the company-wide events?

What does their peer review shows? Are they exceeding expectations or are they only working to meet expectations? We know that these employees will not seek out new career opportunities. What happens when they are forced to do so, involuntarily?

Change does not have to be drastic or life changing for everyone. It can be a gradual process that one eases into. In order to manage change and be receptive to it, you have to want it and be prepared for it. If an employee doesn't want to change, they will resist it every step of the way. They will face the most challenges when they are put in a situation where change is their only option.

Change for an employee can be as singular as learning a new skill or making a request to take on additional assignments. For others, change can be a new career, moving to a new company or even a new city.

When you do decide to change positions or company, be sure that you are taking with you more knowledge and skills, as well as confidence in your abilities based on your accomplishments. It's always a good feeling when you are able to leave with more than what you came with.

Recognize when it's time to move on. We often hear that where we are may or may not be where we are meant to be. When the time comes, it would be helpful to be ready with a workable plan.

Sometimes when God brings us out of a bad situation we are still trying to hold on and look back, instead of forward. We have to know when it's time to make a clean break. We may not know what the future holds, but we do know who holds our future. Let this be your motivation and guide. We cannot move forward if we are still holding on to the past, to the job with no upward mobility, to the manager with tied hands, to employees who are stuck in the past, and to lower compensation.

Change is good when you are looking for it. Many times we have to go through a lot of unpleasant experiences before we can see and appreciate the change. Embrace change and go with the flow. You may end up asking yourself why you took so long, and why you hadn't done this a long time ago.

Don't ever allow yourself to become a disgruntled employee. If you know, think or feel it's time for you to move on to another department or to a different company, do so with grace and with your head held high. Only you know what is best for you.

Again, have a plan and set it in motion. If at all possible, leave on good terms with the folks you worked with in case you want to return. That way, when the interviewer ask you what your former manager or co-workers would say about you, you won't have to break into a sweat before answering. In most cases you will find that you get along better with your former co-workers when you are not competing with them. You will be in a better position to be open, relaxed and develop a friendship.

Don't be afraid of change, or to change. Change represents personal and professional growth. It demonstrates your ability to be flexible and to multitask. Being open to change is an attractive trait if your goal is to achieve career growth. Change is an opportunity to learn and build on your knowledge, and will help you to further your career.

Things do not change, we change. Thoreau, Walden.

Own Your Career

There was a time when qualified individuals didn't have to send out resumes or sit down for job interviews. Their reputation and job skills were well known in the industry. It would only take a phone call for them to move up the ladder or into a new position, or work for a different company.

Imagine you are an Attorney writing briefs, filing motions, trying and winning cases. You may have a research assistant and/or paralegal to do some of the leg work for you. You have been doing this for about 10, 15, or 20 years. You are not a partner, and you are okay with that because it's less pressure on you. You are a specialty attorney specializing in intellectual property, bankruptcy, taxes, corporate law, whatever the case may be. You still have a personal responsibility to be aware of the latest happenings within the legal community.

The same is true for Real Estate Brokers and Agents. The current condition of the economy has changed the spending habits of future buyers as well as the lending and underwriting standards for banks and investors. It's equally important to be aware of these changes and have current knowledge of the market in which you work. Real estate offices have become rental management offices and handling a lot more than showing and selling properties.

In these professional positions, members are required to take annual courses and attend various workshops, seminars and conferences to meet and greet the industry leaders, network with fellow members and learn what's happening in the industry. These are required for maintaining professional licenses and memberships, as well as to gain new knowledge and improve job skills.

Many Real Estate Brokers and Attorneys never change jobs. Their career is a lifetime commitment and they get better at it by working long hours and staying current with their market. People in administrative type positions and non-professional positions need to be doing the same thing.

Take advantage of any and all opportunities being offered by the company. Don't work yourself out of a job by thinking you are too busy to accept that Brown Bag invitation. Or, think that because you've taken the class years ago, you don't need to take it again.

For the record, you don't have to either.

Do you know what separates you from the person sitting next to you? Perhaps there is nothing or at least nothing yet. The difference between who sends out the most resumes and has been unemployed the longest, versus who gets the job may very well be whose skills are more updated.

You may argue that you've been at the same company the longest or you have been doing the job longer, and have more experience. You may be correct in those aspects. But let's break it down to see how you spent the last 10, 15 or 20 plus years you are so proud to mention, versus how your competitor spent the last 3-5 years doing the same job as you.

You have held upwards of three different positions within the company compared to only one for your competitor. You have listed your job responsibilities and the various company activities and events that you oversee, volunteered for and participated in. Breaking it down even further, it would appear that your productive to volunteer work ratio is about 60:40. In addition, your list of accomplishments includes your time volunteering.

In the past year, can you give us an example of one change you were responsible for getting implemented in the department or the company? How do you feel you've contributed to the company's bottom line over the years? Name a new skill that you've recently acquired or a class you've taken.

It's easy to mislead a lot of folks by telling them what you do, but you are only fooling yourself when you have nothing to show for your years of service.

Why spend time making excuses and looking for someone to blame for your current unemployment when you can look for ways to better your situation? If you had a good relationship with your former managers, call them up and ask what they thought your strengths and weaknesses were. Find out what you did well and what additional training they feel will benefit you the most. Include this feedback in your self-assessment to determine your best choice of industry, career or job.

Ask yourself how much effort you put into completing assignments. Are you good at time management and able to complete tasks on time? Do you work well under stress? How much supervision do you need? Are you in the habit of writing things down or do you ask people to repeat what was said? Keep a list of your strengths and weaknesses and refer back to them when applying for new positions.

No matter how secure you feel in your job and the position you hold with the company, keep your resume updated. The employees at Enron were flying high one day and then crashed without seeing it coming. Well, some did. Many employees had a lot of time invested in their jobs. But, how many actually had an updated resume? It's hard to tell. You never want to find yourself having to go back and figure out what you did when you are in a state of vulnerability. By then, you are not sure where to begin especially if you haven't had to job hunt for a number of years.

The process is constantly changing. Having your resume already updated will allow you to post it ahead of others and in front of prospective employers quickly. Too many people panic and breakdown into tears when they get laid-off because they don't know what to do or where to begin. Use your time on the job wisely.

Remember those emails and invitations you kept getting about learning new skills? Well, if you were smart to take advantage of them, you can now add them to your resume and move ahead of the line, and to the top of the pile of potential candidates for hiring.

If you've had 10, 15 or more years of experience doing the same thing at the same company, it may signal you are not open to change and are not flexible. If your responsibilities changed at any time during your employment, you will need to indicate them, even if your job title did not change.

Don't always go after the same types of jobs and don't feel like you have to do the same thing you've been doing for years. Be open to change. Be flexible. Know the current market. There was a time when technology jobs were the hottest and the stock market was booming. When the technology market crashed, it was replaced with real estate jobs and people were buying and selling, and enjoying the American dream. Well, even the real estate market today has seen better days. This is where your ability to be flexible may be tested.

With the shift in the real estate market, for example, there's also a shift in the types of jobs that are available. If you are a licensed Contractor, chances are a lot of your business came from the construction of new homes. With the reduced demand for new construction, an alternative can be repairing and remodeling Bank-Owned properties. There are a lot of homeowners out there not letting their homes go to foreclosure without a fist fight with the dry walls or a kick here and there. Sometimes they are thoughtful enough to leave a written message or mural on the walls.

There's a need for licensed Contractors to complete the remodel started by the evicted homeowners. You may not get the big contracts you were once accustomed to, but there's enough volume to keep your workers busy and to pay the expenses. Be resourceful and creative. Money looks and smell the same so it doesn't matter who it comes from as long as you earned it the good old fashion way.

Why do you think the younger folks get hired over someone with experience? They are more eager to learn and adapt to a career change, and come cheaper.

It's good to have transferrable skills, but do not put yourself in a financial bind where you regress in your career. Too often we see career-focused, qualified individuals in new careers and work in jobs that are out of character for them. These are the same ones who were always sharply dressed in the latest trends, and the proud owners of the newest electronic toys.

The problem is, while they were busy working, they were not managing their own finances. When the regular paychecks stopped, they found themselves scrambling to pay for even their basic expenses. In order to not lose the things they've accumulated, they were forced to accept the first job they were offered. This is a job and pay they would not have otherwise taken.

This is yet another reason why we see companies not hiring qualified individuals who carry a large amount of debt. They may also not hire young people for high salary positions. Companies are looking for qualified and financially responsible workers who they can trust, train and promote to leadership positions to make financial decisions on their behalf.

Financial responsibility is an actual requirement for church members wanting to become Deacons. Financial institutions use this to fill positions that involve the handling of money.

If individuals are not able to manage their own personal finances, would you want them to handle yours? Glenn Shepard said it best, 'Don't take financial advice from people who are broke.'

HIRE YOURSELF

The moment we become unemployed, we get overwhelmed with a range of emotions from sadness and disappointment to anger and resentment. We try to remember what we did and didn't do during our last period of employment, and the people we worked with and for. We look for ways to both accept and disagree with the decision that led to our separation.

It's important that we go through these emotions and not ignore them in order to learn the right questions to ask to get the right answers. We will then need to transfer those emotions into helping decide how, when, where and what to look for in the next job.

Being unemployed involuntarily may be the push we needed to do something different or to follow our passion. Sometimes we get comfortable doing jobs that we have no emotional attachment to or enjoy, but will continue working for the financial stability.

You may be working as a waitress, and spend your days off baking cupcakes and catering to special events. Or, you may be a legal assistant with aspirations to become an attorney. Here, getting laid off and hopefully with a severance package, can give you the boost to go after your dream. You are no longer tied to the full time job which was holding you back. You know the market and the industry well, so the only thing now that's preventing you from achieving your goal is you. For others, becoming unemployed can be devastating at first and will take longer to accept.

Do you show up at work every day ready to work? Do you have good work ethics? Are you highly motivated and able to work without supervision? Do you know how to lead and motivate others to learn, to get the job done? Do you consider yourself to be skilled and experienced in your career field?

How well do you know the business as a whole? Are you knowledgeable about the industry in which you work? Do you know the industry leaders and their competition? Do you find yourself working twice as hard and more than anyone else and only getting half the credit, if any?

We often hear that if we keep doing the same thing, we'll get the same results. Why continue looking for someone to hire you for your skills when you can hire yourself? Start your own business. Market yourself and the services you can provide. Not everyone may be in a position to make such a drastic change, but it's worth considering. You may also consider taking on a partner or group of friends with complementary skills, and who are looking for employment.

One of the first things to do is take an inventory of your skills. List everything you've done over the years, the tools, applications and systems you've worked with. Consider your knowledge of the market you want to penetrate. List the things you are passionate about and where your strengths are. What companies do you know who can use your skills on a short-term or long-term basis?

What if you were so sure you were going to get hired by a particular company and it didn't happen? You have all the skills and qualifications the position required and you felt you will fit well in the company and be able to contribute immediately. The interview went well. You were on time. You asked the right questions and were satisfied with the responses you gave. Yet, after waiting for the call, none came.

Why not call each company back where you felt you would be able to provide what they were looking for? Let them know that you are very interested in working with them and felt after the interview you were a good fit. Find out if they've filled the position and if so, why you were not selected.

Is it possible that the interviewer felt the same way, but after further consideration felt they could not afford your salary and benefits? Or, what if they only needed someone to work on a specific project and will not need to add someone full time? What if after listening to you and what you can do for them, they realized that they may need to do some reorganization to utilize their current staff?

The only way to find out the reasons why is to ask. Here, you can get first-hand information as to what companies are really looking for and you can create your own niche of services for them. Show how you can help them streamline their services to be more efficient. Most companies utilize outside expertise to help do this. Or, you may be able to assist on an Information Technology project or a Marketing Campaign. You can offer your expertise as a paid consultant.

If you are leaning toward becoming self-employed, search the Internet for small business ideas with low start-up costs that you can do. Look for legitimate jobs you can do from home. Set a budget and make a business plan. Your local *Small Business Administration* website can be a resource. They offer free online training, local counseling and mentoring.

If, for example, you love children and enjoy teaching them, you may consider opening up your own Child Care Center. Do your research to find out all you need to know and do to get started. Create a business plan to include the number of kids and ages you are able to care for, your hours of operation, the ideal location and whether you will need an assistant. Include your rates, expected income and expenses. Find out about the state licensing and inspection requirements for this type of business and any additional training and certifications for you and your assistant, such as CPR.

Many small businesses are started by people who had a single idea. They may have found the solution to a problem, or they may be looking to capitalize on a hobby. Becoming your own boss may be a great way to solve your unemployment situation. Let everyone in your social and professional groups know what services you can offer and how they can contact you. Ask them to help you spread the word.

Advertise your new company on *LinkedIn*. Contact recruiters and agencies you have worked with in the past and let them know your availability and change in status. You can still be flexible and open to full-time or part-time employment. Do what works best for you. Make good use of your time and qualifications.

Finally, always have a back-up plan.

Individual
Responsibility

There is an opportunity and job for everyone. It may not look the way we envisioned it to be right at the start, but over time and with hard work it can become something we enjoy doing. We need to exercise patience and not expect immediate success. Success is earned only after we have dedicated our time into learning, performing and expanding our knowledge of the job and the business. We can declare success when we have exceeded our individual goals and are contributing to company's bottom line. Value the contributions you make to the company, not how much you are paid.

What do parents tell their children when they want to drop out of school or they may be failing a class because they do not like the teacher? Or, they think a particular teacher just does not like them. Whereas teachers have a responsibility to teach and educate every child they are entrusted to in the classroom, it is the student's responsibility to learn and do well in school. That is their job. The child's reward would be to graduate from each grade level and eventually obtain their diploma to show for it.

Teachers cannot teach everything that children need to learn to become successful in life. That additional learning has to come from other areas such as family members, the library, extracurricular activities, community centers like the YMCA, after school tutoring and the church. This is no different to learning in the work place. We always have to find other ways to develop ourselves to reach our full potential and not wait to be told what to do.

If you do not have the type of manager who shares new info on a regular basis, then you will have to take the initiative to ask questions and do your own research. You may often have to go outside your group for help, thereby expanding your areas of knowledge and resources. The skills you learn will help you each time you have to start a new job.

Therefore, you should never go to work expecting someone to hold your hand. The last thing you want is someone spoon-feeding you what they want you to do and know. In so doing, you will become dependent on them for more answers each time something doesn't work out the way they said it should. You have to learn to think outside the office cube and ask the 'what if' questions.

Remember, folks can only teach you what they know. Eventually, all the spoon feeding will leave a bitter taste in your mouth. You will have to start looking to someone else who can point you in the right direction, and show you how to be resourceful. Anything less will hinder how well and how quickly you learn the job and adapt to changes as they come. Once you succeed at this, keep on learning and leave the spoon feeders behind.

One other thing to keep in mind about spoon feeders, the information they share may not always be accurate and up-to-date. These are the folks who resisted change. You will always hear them say 'what used to happen,' but they can't tell you what is happening now. They are stuck in the past and would prefer you do only what they taught you.

This is when you reach the fork in the road. The good thing is it becomes your responsibility to choose the path to your success or to please the folks you work with. You have to ask yourself and answer the tough questions like what is your purpose for being there. Are the people I want to please my friends and family? Do they want to see me succeed or are they afraid of my success because they refuse to change and accept change? You always have to do what's best for you—always.

Any work relationship that does not drive you to be your best and to be successful should be limited, and avoided if possible. They are a distraction and should be seen as just that. Stay focus on your personal and professional goals. Surround yourself with positive people. Stay on topic and don't get sucked into idle talk.

Know when you've done a good job. Don't wait for your manager or someone else to recognize it and tell you that. If your manager does not value your hard work or make your achievements visible to others, it then becomes your responsibility to do so if necessary.

We are responsible for our personal and professional career development. Do not wait on anyone to tell you what you need to do. Ask for suggestions and solicit feedback, but the final decision must be yours.

Don't be afraid to admit that you don't know something. If you want to learn, you have to be honest with those who have offered to help you. You don't want people making the wrong assumptions about you. The result can be a costly decision or a wasted effort. At the same time, share your knowledge with others and they will share with you, even the baby boomers. We hope.

Unless you take the time to step back and be willing to make the necessary adjustments in your life, you will not improve personally, professionally or economically. If you keep doing the same things and continue making the same mistakes, you will remain stuck. You have a choice of ten fingers to point to anyone to blame for you not getting hired or moving ahead in your career. Be sure to reserve one of those fingers for yourself.

Take a personal inventory of your skills, knowledge, abilities and competencies. Find where the gaps are. Determine what's current and what's needed. Ask, what am I doing to safeguard my stake in the company?

Are you working hard or hardly working? Do you feel you are contributing to the department goals? What about the company's bottom line? Do you know your department's goals and priorities? What do you need from your manager to be more effective and efficient, and to move into a new role? Know what to expect from your manager. Have high expectations for yourself.

Watch your body language and speech when you are communicating with others. What signals are you sending to your manager regarding your interest in moving into a leadership role?   Be sure to communicate your readiness and preparedness for the new role or new job. Know when to speak and when it's time to listen.

Do you show up to meetings prepared and on-time? Are you in tune with what's going on during the meeting or are you leading a separate discussion? There's a time and place for everything. If you do not have any input to share during the meetings, try asking questions to show your interest. Take notes and be attentive.

Let your dress reflect your professional persona and self-confidence. Show that you believe in the vision and mission of the company you work for and follow the company's dress code. If you work in a casual environment, dress in such a way for you to stand out from the crowd and to differentiate yourself from the regular customers.

Know that when you are in a place where business is conducted, your attire should signal your professionalism and approachability.   You want what you say and do to be taken seriously. This is one way to gain respect and to build trust with customers and associates.

We need to create a balance between our work and personal life. Be mindful of personal issues you are tempted to share. In sharing, we may be transferring the burdens of those issues to our co-workers. This can be emotionally draining and will adversely affect work productivity and efforts to build friendships. Our goal should be to keep the workplace professional and positive.

It is our individual responsibility to be ready to work when we walk through the office doors. Learn to pace yourself so the day is spent learning and being productive.   Set daily goals for what you want to accomplish.   Whether you are writing a letter or selling a product, be the best writer and the best salesperson you can be. Every accomplishment, no matter how big or small, is an opportunity to improve your job skills and increase your knowledge of the industry you work in. Your goal should be to successfully complete every task you started and to achieve the expected results.

If you are not in the habit of finishing anything you've started and if you do not feel you are learning anything new on the job, you may be escalating your departure or aiming to fire yourself. You will also not have any accomplishments to add to your resume or be able to demonstrate what you did on the job.

Unless this is part of your exit strategy plan, consider setting smaller goals that you can accomplish within a set time frame, and build from there. Go to the company's online university (if there's one) for courses that can improve your knowledge and skills. Make time to complete them. You need to always be preparing for unemployment and career advancement.

It's a good idea to know the best time to quit. We are surrounded by people, objects, rules and regulations that affect us directly and indirectly, and for which we have only some control over. We may feel compelled to remain in our current position even though we don't feel valued by the manager, are under-paid, and have to deal with personality conflicts. Consider switching to a different team or company. Find a new position, particularly one with growth potential that utilizes your skills and abilities. The longer you remain is no guarantee of the work environment becoming less toxic or hostile.

When preparing to enter a new workplace, remind yourself of the job you were hired to perform and the expectations. Be considerate and know that your actions and inactions directly affect others.   Do not waste other people's time and don't steal the company's time. If you need help, ask for it.   If you don't know how do to something, admit it. If you ever feel overwhelmed, take a break then go back and prioritize what needs to be done.

Be friendly to everyone you meet and keep an open mind. Remember your manager is your boss, not your friend. Keep the relationship as such to avoid any discomposure when soliciting feedback on your performance.

Maintain a positive attitude. Show up always ready to work and make every day a productive day.

I wish you success in your job search and on the job.

INDIVIDUAL WORKSHOPS

Problem 1: Not feeling challenged in current position.

Cause: Worked in the same job for a number of years without any change in job responsibilities.

Goal: Need something new to focus on.

Action:

1. Do a self-assessment to determine your strengths and weakness, skills, gaps and training needs.

2. Search the company's website for other positions within the company.

3. Verify your qualifications for the new position.

4. Have a conversation with your manager and ask for additional assignments or a new role.

5. Have realistic expectations and envision yourself in the new job.

6. Learn a new skill and request additional training.

7. Speak with associates in other departments and find out what they do.

8.   Ask your Manager to allow you to cross train with other team members and with others in another department.

9.   Read this book--Why Qualified People Don't Get Hired or Stay with the Company (based on an employee's perspective and experiences).

Problem 2: Currently unemployed and actively seeking employment.

Cause: Laid-off from last company due to position being outsourced.

Goal: Obtain full time employment in the same industry.

Action:

1.   Do a self-assessment to determine your strengths and weakness, skills, gaps and training needs.

2.   Target companies within the industry you are interested in.

3.   Determine the size of the company you are comfortable with.

4.   Establish an acceptable salary range for negotiations.

5.   Post resumes to multiple online job search sites.

6.   Search company websites for current openings.

7.   Search Temporary Services Agency sites for their list of client companies.

8.   Link-up with your social groups and network.

9.   Prepare yourself and be available for phone and in-person interview. Find a partner and practice answering interview questions.

10.   Research the company to familiarize yourself with what they do and how long they've been in business. Find out who the CEO of the company is.

11.   Read this book--Why Qualified People Don't Get Hired or Stay with the Company (based on an employee's perspective and experiences).

Epilogue

Because employment is 'at will', many of us go to work every day wondering if today will be our last. It can be difficult to perform with this thought at the back of our mind. It's easier when we can see the writing on the wall as it gives us the opportunity to prepare and explore other options. There is no excuse for ignorance. Pay attention to the warning signs as unemployment may one day become our reality.

Even though we are employed, we may be underemployed. Use this time to decide whether, and for how long you want to stay in your current position. You may have accepted this position on a temporary basis. Check-in with your current recruiter or placement agency for a new assignment once the contract ends.

Always prepare yourself for unemployment. Keep your resume and job references updated. Make sure you have at least six months of savings to carry you through to make up the deficiency of the unemployment compensation.

If you plan to leave your current position, be sure you have a new and better position to go to before quitting. Your previous salary becomes irrelevant when you become unemployed. The likelihood of getting another job with the same salary or more in this economy is rare.

Do not feel you were making too much money to consider employment with the Temporary Services Agencies. Be consistent and aggressive in your job search.

Know there's value in your education, skills, experience and knowledge of the industry that employers are looking for. Make your resume available to as many of them as possible. Utilize all the free online tools and resources available, including your network of friends. Be confident in yourself and what you can contribute to employers.

If you've never had a manager that took the time to mentor and develop employees, find ways to motivate yourself to learn all you can about the job and the industry. If you are going to follow a leader, know where they are leading you. Or, become the leader.

Focus on yourself and what you are trying to accomplish. Set both short and long-term goals, and work towards achieving them. Be responsible for your success. Let the work you do demonstrate what you are capable of doing, as well as your potential. Stay motivated by rewarding yourself after you've accomplished each goal--very important.

We are working in a competitive environment and must align ourselves with the needs of the company in order to stand out. Grow and change as the company grows and goes through changes. It is your individual responsibility to know yourself, your strength, to find your passion. Always do your best and feel proud of your accomplishments.

Managers, Supervisors and Leaders, your qualified, talented and high performers have a message for you. Do not take them for granted because they are self-motivated, college-educated and results-oriented. They want you to show them once in a while that you appreciate what they do for you.

What they need most is to be included, to feel empowered and do work that is both intellectually challenging and meaningful. Their retention is dependent on it.

WORKS CITED AND REFERENCED

ABC News Nightline. iFactory: Inside Apple. Anchor. Bill Weir. 21 Feb 2012 and 22 Feb 2012.

AON Hewitt. www.AON.com. Trends in Global Employee Engagement. 2011.

Baur, John. www.stcroixsource.com. JFL Eliminates 85 Jobs for CNAs, LPNs. 28 Feb 2012.

Celebrity Apprentice. Host. Donald Trump. www.nbc.com. NBC is a Media and Entertainment Company.

CNN Online. www.cnn.com. CNN is a Cable News Network.

Cohan, William. Author. Money and Power: How Goldman Sachs came to Rule the World. 2011.

Cottrell, David. Listen Up, Leader! Pay attention, Improve and Guide. Second Edition. 2000.

LinkedIn. www.linkedin.com. LinkedIn is the world's largest professional network on the Internet.

Restaurant Impossible. Host. Robert Irvine. Food Network. Food Network is a Food Network program.

Robison, Jennifer. "Turning Around Employee Turnover: Costly churn can be reduced if managers know what to look for—and they usually don't." <u>Gallup Management Journal.</u> 2012.

Shepard, Glenn. Glenn is an Author and Speaker in Nashville.

Smith, Greg. Letter. Why I am Leaving Goldman Sachs. <u>The New York Times.</u> 3 March 2012.

<u>Tabatha's Salon Takeover</u>. Host. Tabatha Coffey. www.bravotv.com Bravo is a Program Service of NBCUniversal, a Media and Entertainment Company.

U.S. Bureau of Labor Statistics. www.bls.gov. The Bureau of Labor Statistics is a part of the U.S. Department of Labor.

U.S. Census Bureau. www.census.gov. The Census Bureau is a part of the U.S. Department of Commerce.

U.S. Small Business Administration. www.sba.gov.

Undercover Boss (International) Abroad. www.tlc.com. TLC is part of the Discovery family of television networks, the World's #1 Non-fiction Media Company.

Wagner, Rodd, and Harter, James K. "The Twelfth Element of Great Management: Employees don't outgrow the need to learn and grow." <u>Gallup Management Journal</u>. Dec 2006.

ABOUT THE AUTHOR

This is the first book for Molita Powell. Her career has taken her from San Diego, California to Dallas, Texas. She has worked in small, medium and large companies across several industries and witnessed the growth, re-organization and demise of some of those companies. Others are struggling to keep up with competition and with the changing tides of the economy.

www.ingramcontent.com/pod-product-compliance
Lightning Source LLC
Chambersburg PA
CBHW051509170526
45166CB00001B/456

* 9 7 8 1 4 7 8 2 3 5 1 1 8 *